GLOBAL WARMING

A scientific and biblical expose'
of climate change

1:1

answersingenesis.org
believing it. defending it. proclaiming it.

ISBN: 1-60092-212-X

Printed in the United States of America

www.answersingenesis.org

GL🌐BAL WARMING

A scientific and biblical exposé
of climate change

THE TOP 5 CLAIMS OF CLIMATE CHANGE ALARMISTS • EYE-OPENING CHARTS AND
GRAPHS • BONUS ARTICLES • AN OVERVIEW OF BIBLICALLY-BASED ENVIRONMENTAL
STEWARDSHIP • FULL TRANSCRIPT FROM THE DOCUMENTARY

Table of Contents

Introduction

Global warming is a controversial subject that is often misunderstood, both by scientists and the public. There is no doubt that it has become the number one environmental issue of the twenty-first century. But what is a Christian to think of global warming? Does the Bible have anything to say about environmental issues? What does the science actually tell us about climate change? Are we on the brink of global disasters and irreversible damage to our environment? Should we take immediate drastic measures to decrease our "carbon footprint"?

This pocket guide answers those questions. Here you will find a discussion of what the Bible has to say about our relationship with creation, and how a Christian should approach environmental issues such as global warming. We will also examine the evidence for and against man-caused global warming.

More than ever, Christians need to think biblically about every area of our lives. We must examine everything carefully in light of God's Word and respond appropriately. It is our prayer that this pocket guide will help you do just that.

Creation and Conservation

By Ken Ham

*P*eople today are becoming more and more concerned with the environment and what humans are doing to it. Many are expressing alarm about global warming, predicting a dire future for us and our children. For millions, including many Christians, how we care for the environment has become a very emotional issue.

For instance, at one of AiG's seminars that I was conducting, I was talking about pre-evangelism—establishing the need for destroying the stumbling block of evolution in people's thinking so they will listen to the gospel. To illustrate the point, I showed a slide depicting trees and rocks (representing the barrier of evolution) being cleared by a bulldozer.

At the end of the session, one young man, in an emotional response, described this slide as anti-environmental, and insisted I should stop using it! Perhaps you have heard of the environmental group which advocates violent destruction of earth-moving equipment to protect the earth. I don't know if this person was from this evolutionary, New-Age group, but he seemed to have been influenced by their ideas.

I thought of questions I could have asked: "Is there any wood in the house you live in? Do you drive on roads made after clearing trees? Have you ever heated yourself with a wood fire?" Thankfully, I held my tongue, but the more I thought about it, the more I realized that my illustration (which used the clearing of land only as an analogy) could tend to offend needlessly those deeply concerned about the environment.

Rather than emotionally responding to environmental issues, such as global warming, we need to develop a Christian environmental ethic. To do this, we must have a foundation on which to build this ethic, and this foundation must be the Word of God. And, as with other issues, we ultimately end up back in the Book of Genesis—the book of beginnings—to build our thinking and to develop a truly Christian viewpoint and plan of action.

Who owns the world?

"In the beginning God created the heavens and the earth." The fact that God created the world means He owns it. In light of this, surely we can hardly claim ownership of anything. Psalm 95:5 states, "The sea is His, for He made it; and His hands formed the dry land." In Psalm 24:1, we read, "The earth is the Lord's, and all its fullness." Everything we have has come from God, who created all things. Because we don't own the creation, this also means we have no right to exploit it—for example, use it to make a profit for pure greed, without considering the glory of God, the good of the creation, and the needs of our fellow man.

Who has the right to rule over the earth?

In Genesis 1:28, God told Adam and Eve to "Be fruitful and multiply; fill the earth and subdue it; have dominion over the fish of the sea, over the birds of the air, and over every living thing that moves on the earth." Genesis 2:15 states, "Then the Lord God took the man and put him in the garden of Eden to tend and keep it."

God created humans different from the animals, with a superior brain and the ability to communicate information from one generation to the next, that we might subdue the earth and have dominion over it, as commanded. We therefore have a special responsibility, and are expected to care for what has been entrusted to us by our Creator.

How is God concerned for the creation?

In Matthew 6:28–29, God tells us that He clothes the lilies of the field so that "even Solomon in all his glory was not arrayed like one of these." Not even a sparrow falls without God's knowledge and permission. If God is so concerned about living things, surely man, His steward, must be similarly concerned. We should then want to eliminate or minimize needless harm to the world and its occupants.

Why are there "green" crises?

When God made the world, everything at first was "very good," or "perfect" (Genesis 1:31; Deuteronomy 32:4). All living things were in perfect harmony, with a sinless man tending the perfect creation.

However, that is not the situation now. Romans 8:22 tells us "the whole creation groans and labors with birth pangs together until now." Genesis 3 records the event that led to this sad state of affairs, with all living things and all world systems decaying and dying.

Romans 5:12 explains that man's actions (disobedience to God's command not to eat of the forbidden fruit) led to sin, which resulted in God's cursing the world with death. Genesis 3:17–19 describes some of the ways this sin affected the creation. "Cursed is the ground for your sake; in toil you shall eat of it all the days of your life. Both thorns and thistles it shall bring forth for you. . . . In the sweat of your face you shall eat bread."

The whole of creation is now running down and wearing out. "The earth will grow old like a garment" (Isaiah 51:6), and man's sinful nature has disrupted the relationship with the environment.

The sin of Adam, which we all inherit, was one of rebellion against God's rules, and man, ever since, has made his own rules. This results in selfishness (and therefore exploitation), the refusal to practice love towards our fellow man and other creatures, as well as poor stewardship of God's creation, and man's desire to serve his own personal ends.

Benefit from wise stewardship

Deuteronomy 25:4 states: "You shall not muzzle an ox while it treads out the grain." In Isaiah 5 and John 15, God shows that even He expects fruit or "profit" from His work. In other words, there is benefit to be gained from wise stewardship.

But man is not a perfect steward any more. Even though the resources God created are there for our use, man often exploits these resources at the expense of his fellow man, and causes needless loss and destruction of other parts of God's creation. Surely this is wrong!

Conversely, much of the emphasis of the modern conservation movement and global warming alarmists is evolutionary and pantheistic, worshipping the creature rather than the Creator (Romans 1). This ignores the biblical mandate to rule over the earth and subdue it. The development of energy sources (coal, natural gas, petroleum, atomic power, etc.), the mining of mineral resources, the cutting of timber for building, etc., is not wrong. Ecclesiastes 3:1–8 states that there is a time to plant and a time to uproot, a time to kill and a time to heal, a time to tear down and a time to build, a time to keep and a time to throw away, a time for war and a time for peace. It is the abuse of these resources—the exploitation, the waste, the greed, and the haste—that is wrong.

Proverbs 12:10 says, "A righteous man regards the life of his animal, but the tender mercies of the wicked are cruel." Dominion means to rule, to administer, to work, and to take care of the creation—not to lord over it in a tyrannical manner, or to needlessly destroy it.

What should the Christian do about this?

Some say that Christians can cut down a tree to build a house, or burn timber to keep warm, but must not just destroy it for the sake of cutting down a tree. Some say that Christians can kill animals for food, but should not just slaughter them for sport.

But then, if controlled deer-hunting or kangaroo-killing were not allowed, many more animals would suffer for various and complicated reasons. Because this is no longer a perfect world, there would be harm to their own kind and others. In the right circumstances, if mature timber is harvested properly, there is no net loss, even if the timber is not simply used for housing, for example. If it is not harvested, the forest may become unhealthy and fire-prone without proper forest management. This would all be part of using the earth's resources as God intended in telling man to rule over the earth and subdue it.

The global warming "problem" has similar issues to address. If harsh measure are enacted to reduce carbon emissions, the costs to industry will be passed on to consumers, raising even further the price of energy and food, and causing hardship to millions of people in developing countries. And as you will see in this handbook, the science behind global warming is not settled, and trying to stop global warming may do much more harm than good.

A warning

It is natural to want to see things in black and white terms. And there certainly are black and white issues. However, some things are so varied and complex, often involving sinful human behavior and motives, that black and white answers may be risky and hard to find. Sincere, Bible-believing Christians may end up on opposing sides of such issues.

Regarding issues like global warming, uranium mining, logging, etc., we usually have more questions than answers. Often we do not have enough information to ask the right questions. We need to gather and carefully assess all the information possible in our attempt to resolve these issues. Sometimes it will be a matter of weighing competing rights and wrongs, which will give rise to different answers for different situations. Use of a resource might be right for one area, circumstance, or time, and wrong for another. Instead of blanket rules applied indiscriminately, we must fall back on principles.

Most of all, we need to continue to adopt and develop a Christian environmental ethic based on the Bible, and we need to practice it. We need to take dominion, ruling over the earth and subduing it, gaining fruit for our labor, all the while understanding that our own sinful nature may blind us, and we must reject wanton and needless exploitation of the creation for selfish gain. There will be no better solution to the environmental crisis until God makes a new heaven and a new earth in which "righteousness dwells" (2 Peter 3:13).

Ken Ham
*President and CEO, Answers in Genesis–USA
& the Creation Museum*

Ken's bachelor's degree in applied science (with an emphasis on environmental biology) was awarded by the Queensland Institute of Technology in Australia. He also holds a diploma of education from the University of Queensland. In recognition of the contribution Ken has made to the church in the USA and internationally, Ken has been awarded two honorary doctorates: a Doctor of Divinity (1997) from Temple Baptist College in Cincinnati, Ohio and a Doctor of Literature (2004) from Liberty University in Lynchburg, Virginia.

Since moving to America in 1987, Ken has become one of the most in-demand Christian conference speakers and talk show guests in America. He has appeared on national shows such as Fox's *The O'Reilly Factor* and *Fox and Friends in the Morning*; CNN's *The Situation Room with Wolf Blitzer*, ABC's *Good Morning America*, the BBC, *CBS News Sunday Morning*, *The NBC Nightly News with Brian Williams*, and *The PBS News Hour with Jim Lehrer*.

Global Warming in Perspective

by Melinda Christian

These days it seems you can hardly turn on the TV, go online, or open your morning newspaper without being confronted with the idea of global warming. In his 2006 Oscar-winning documentary *An Inconvenient Truth*, former U.S. Vice President Al Gore presents global warming as an imminent threat to the planet and paints an alarming picture of a future in which mankind ultimately destroys life on earth.

But global warming is far more complex than one 96-minute film can convey, and most people are simply not getting some of the most important information.

How do we approach the subject of global warming?

It's clear that global warming is a complex and emotionally charged issue, one that cannot be ignored in today's cultural and political climate. New claims and counter-claims appear in the press with numbing regularity, leaving many Christians uncertain what to believe. Rather than getting lost in the details, it is necessary first to uncover the basic facts and then to understand the assumptions that drive the interpretations of those facts.

Although many people may think otherwise, all of us have assumptions (beliefs) that influence how we look at the facts. If a scientist believes in billions of years of earth history, he will assume, for example, that polar ice needed hundreds of thousands of years to build up over two miles in depth. Scientists who believe in the biblical account of Noah's Flood, on the other hand, believe the ice must have appeared shortly after the Flood. Depending on their assumptions, equally skilled scientists can reach very different conclusions.

In the global warming debate, it is important to separate fact from interpretation. We hear a great deal about the dangers of CO_2 emissions and greenhouse gases, but rarely do we hear the facts behind the hype.

Even "facts" need to be qualified. For example, NASA has reported that the average number of major hurricanes (categories 4 and 5) has doubled since 1970. But this is "selective data sorting." When you calculate the average of all hurricanes, you find much less of an increase. In fact, the year 2007 saw a decrease in hurricanes. So NASA's "fact" may be true, but it is not the whole truth.

Global warming's top five claims: fact or fiction?

Let's examine the basic facts and assumptions behind each major claim about global warming:

Claim #1: Global warming is really happening.

Global warming *is* really happening, in the strictest definition of the term. According to the National Climatic Data Center, the average global surface temperature has risen approximately 1.2°F (0.7°C) since 1880 (Figure 1). However, this fact alone does not tell us the causes of the warming.

Claim #2: We are causing global warming.

The challenge is to separate natural and human causes, especially

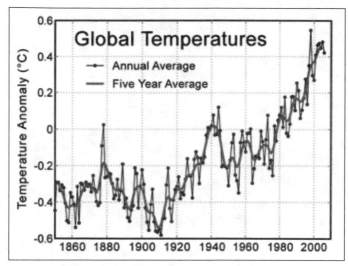

Figure 1. Measurements from the National Climatic Data Center show an increase of global temperatures of about 0.7°C over the past 150 years. Source: Global Warming Art, globalwarmingart.com/wiki/Image:Instrumental_Temperature_Record_png

when we still know so little about the factors in climate change.

It helps to get some historical perspective. We know from Scripture that the worldwide Flood changed the earth's climate dramatically, and ocean sediments indicate that plate tectonics during the Flood had greatly heated the oceans, rising to a temperature at least 36°F (20°C) warmer than today's oceans.[1] Temperatures dropped dramatically as the earth entered an Ice Age.

Since the Ice Age, the earth's temperature has fluctuated by only a few degrees. For example, a medieval "warm period" (AD 900 to 1300) was followed by a "little ice age" (1300 to 1880), when the overall temperature dropped about 2°F (1.2°C) (Figure 2).

These relatively recent fluctuations can be correlated to natural changes, such as volcanic eruptions and cycles in the sun's radiation. (When the earth receives more energy from the sun, the earth gets warmer.) It is logical to assume that similar factors

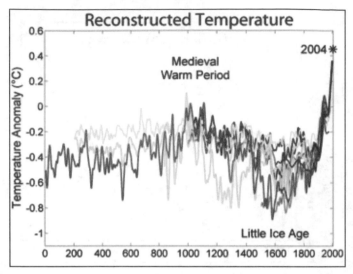

Figure 2. A comparison of 10 different published reconstructions of mean temperature changes during the last 2,000 years, showing the Medieval Warm Period and the Little Ice Age. Source: Global Warming Art, globalwarmingart.com/wiki/ Image:2000_Year_Temperature_Comparison_png

continue to have some influence on today's global warming.

What about human causes of global warming? Alarmists would have us believe that increased CO_2 emissions have triggered global warming. But it is important to understand greenhouse gases. Basically, these are gases in the earth's atmosphere that regulate temperature by holding in heat from the sun, and as such these gases are necessary for life. The primary greenhouse gas, which is responsible for the vast majority of the greenhouse effect, is water vapor. Carbon dioxide, the second most common greenhouse gas, provides only a tiny fraction of the greenhouse effect.

It is certainly true that the burning of fossils fuels is pumping more and more CO_2 into the atmosphere, but it does not necessarily follow that these gases are the sole *cause* of the warming.

In fact, higher concentrations of CO_2 may be, in part, a *result* of warmer temperatures. The oceans have much more CO_2 than the atmosphere, and when the oceans warm up, the CO_2 escapes into the atmosphere. (We see a similar effect when we see gas bubbling out of a glass of warm Coke.)

We have much more to learn about climate change. But looking at the current evidence, it seems very likely that both natural and human factors are at fault, perhaps as much as 50-50.[2]

Claim #3: Global warming will cause many animals and plants to go extinct.

Al Gore's documentary presents viewers with a computer-animated polar bear treading water, struggling to find rest on the last, thin shelf of ice, which breaks apart under his weight. It is an image expressly designed to provoke emotion in the viewer. Polar bears, in reality, are currently thriving.

Receding glaciers, melting ice caps, and other changes are, of course, likely to affect a variety of animal and plant species. But based on the fossil record, it appears that many species, such as the *Miohippus* (a small three-toed, woodland horse) and the woolly mammoth, flourished in the changing climates after Noah's Flood, and eventually went extinct. Humans clearly had nothing to do with these climate changes and extinctions.

According to some climate models, which use current data and a variety of assumptions to predict future climate patterns, several plant and animal species could go extinct by 2050 due to climate change. Currently, however, there are no documented extinctions resulting from global warming.

Claim #4: The oceans will rise dramatically in the next century.

This is one of the more alarming claims. In *An Inconvenient Truth* Gore presents a model in which an ice sheet, whether in

Greenland or West Antarctica, slides into the sea, raising the ocean level by 20 feet (6 m) and submerging much of the earth's coastlines, home to 100 million people. The film implies that this will happen within the next 50 years.

While this would certainly be alarming if it were true, no hard scientific evidence exists to back up the prediction. In fact, even Gore's staunchest supporters don't seem to be convinced: www. stopglobalwarming.com claims that the ocean level will rise only six feet in the next hundred years, a substantial difference—but they present no scientific evidence to back up even *their* claim.

Based on climate models, the UN Intergovernmental Panel on Climate Change estimates that ocean levels will rise approximately 16 inches (25 cm) during this century. While this could result in many inconveniences (without proper planning), it is certainly not the "doomsday" that's been so widely predicted. Nor does such a change seem very significant compared to the rapid rise of the oceans in the past—approximately 200–300 feet (60–90 m)—when the ice melted at the end of the Ice Age, flooding the coasts and burying early human settlements after Babel.

Claim #5: Global warming will cause more weather catastrophes.

Global warming has been blamed for increased hurricanes, tornadoes, floods, droughts, and extreme temperatures. But we must keep a few things in mind. First, extreme weather has never been out of the ordinary since Noah's Flood. Secondly, scientists now have satellites and other advanced equipment that can identify and record modern weather events that would have gone unrecorded in the past, making it difficult to validate whether these events have been increasing.

While the number of hurricanes has increased in recent decades, a recent study in the journal *Nature Geoscience* concludes that global warming is not to blame for increased hurricanes and, in fact, hurricanes are likely to decrease by the end of the century.[3]

Currently, there is insufficient evidence to clearly identify global warming as the cause of extreme weather events.

Christians are reacting in very different ways to the issue of global warming—from finding practical ways to reduce their "carbon footprint" to lobbying the government for action, or ignoring the issue altogether. So what is a biblical approach?

Understanding human "dominion"

When God gave Adam dominion over the earth, he was told to take care of the garden. In verse after verse of Scripture, we learn that God made us stewards of His earth, caretakers of the natural resources that He has provided on this planet. "The earth is the Lord's, and all its fullness" (Psalm 24:1).

But does this mean that we are to protect nature at any cost?

God did not create human beings merely to serve or "preserve" the earth. Rather, He made us in His image, as His highest creation, and He gave us the privilege and duty to glorify Him in everything we do, including managing the earth to make it more beautiful and productive. Just as God "planted a garden," we want to be good gardeners, too.

The earth was made as our dwelling place, and while it is our responsibility to maintain it, we must not place higher importance on the environment than on the people who inhabit it. The Industrial Revolution, so often vilified by global warming activists, has improved the quality of life for millions, even billions, of people. It has also "saved" the lives of untold millions

Weighing our actions

Whatever action we take, whether as individuals or through government action, we must carefully weigh the consequences. While many people support laws to reduce CO_2 emissions, believing that this will appreciably slow the progress of global warming, we must consider whether the science supports this claim. We must also beware of unintended consequences, such as the loss of personal liberties.

Whatever a person's view of the government's role, it is undeniable that laws to limit CO_2 output would have far-reaching effects on the poor. The increased costs of producing food, powering vehicles, and heating and cooling homes are only a few of the potential negative results. Lower-income families, especially in less-developed countries, would be hit especially hard.

E. Calvin Beisner, a respected environmental expert, examines the economic side-effects of anti–CO_2 policies and concludes: "The policies that are being promoted to fight global warming not only will not make a difference . . . but also will have a great harmful impact on the world's poor."[4]

According to Beisner, even the vast changes proposed by global warming activists would have only a negligible effect on CO_2 levels in the atmosphere, with little possibility of reversing or even slowing global warming. But if the proposed changes become reality, the potential costs in lives and freedoms would be incalculable.

But should we do nothing to fight global warming? There are practical things individuals can do to maintain our planet and keep it beautiful and safe for the next generation, such as reducing waste, recycling, and driving fuel-efficient vehicles. The choice to take any of these—or stronger—measures should always be based on a clear understanding of the facts and the eternal principles in God's Word.

God's Word tells us about a "new heaven and a new earth" that He is planning for His people, free of sin and the Curse. Our current environmental problems are serious and worth further thought and action, but the Bible puts all such issues into proper perspective. While we need to behave wisely in the fleeting moments we have on this earth, a much greater change is coming, one that should modify our behavior—the "global warming" described in 2 Peter 3:10. "But the day of the Lord will come as a thief in the night, in which the heavens will pass away with a great noise, and the elements will melt with fervent heat; both the earth and the works that are in it will be burned up."

[1] S. A. Austin et al., "Catastrophic Plate Tectonics: A Global Flood Model of Earth History," in R. E. Walsh, ed. *Proceedings of the Third International Conference on Creationism* (Pittsburgh: Creation Science Fellowship, 1994), p. 615.

[2] After reviewing the scientific literature, meteorologist Mike Oard estimates that natural causes account for about 50% of surface temperature increases since 1880.

[3] Thomas R. Knutson et al., "Simulated Reduction in Atlantic Hurricane Frequency under Twenty-First-Century Warming Conditions," *Nature Geoscience*, May 18, 2008, pp. 359–364.

[4] D. James Kennedy and E. Calvin Beisner, *Overheated: A Reasoned Look at the Global Warming Debate* (Ft. Lauderdale, Florida: Coral Ridge Ministries, 2007), p. 23.

Melinda Christian
Answers in Genesis–USA

Melinda has been a staff member of Answers in Genesis–USA since 2001. She graduated from Calvary Bible College in Kansas City, Missouri. Melinda is an avid writer. She regularly contributes to *Answers* magazine, and is also involved in editing AiG publications.

Human-Caused Global Warming Slight So Far

by Michael Oard

We are constantly bombarded with bad news about global warming. Hurricanes are increasing in frequency and intensity, the Greenland and Antarctic Ice Sheets are melting and raising the sea level, the Arctic Sea ice cap is melting, droughts are imminent, people are dying of the heat, and so on.[1] Global warming will even cause larger and more toxic poison ivy.[2] It is all because man is polluting the atmosphere with carbon dioxide from the burning of fossil fuels and the destruction of tropical forests. We must act now, advocates claim, or we will become engulfed in a runaway heat blast. This is the doomsayers' position.

Other voices allege that global warming will halt the ocean heat circulation in the Atlantic and plunge the earth into the next ice age, which is due soon. Already, the North Atlantic poleward heat transport has supposedly decreased 30%![3]

There are also a number of scientists who believe global warming, so far, has been slight. They believe that doomsayers have not proven their case for the expected huge temperature increase for a doubling of carbon dioxide, and that increased carbon dioxide may have a net beneficial effect. In fact, 20,000 scientists, of whom about 2,700 of them are physicists, geophysicists, climatologists, meteorologists, oceanographers, or environmental scientists, who are in a position to understand the global warming issues, have signed the following statement:

"There is no convincing scientific evidence that human release of carbon dioxide, methane, or other greenhouse gasses is causing or will, in the foreseeable future, cause catastrophic heating of the earth's atmosphere and disruption of the earth's climate. Moreover, there is substantial scientific evidence that increases in atmospheric carbon dioxide produce many beneficial effects upon the natural plant and animal environments of the earth."[4]

I also advocate this position and further reasoned research, providing a forum for the views of both advocates and dissenters of extreme human-caused global warming.[5]

Because of all the bad news and variable positions on the issue, it is no wonder that confusion seems to be rampant. Polls indicate that most people have become convinced that global warming is a serious problem. This is likely due to media bombardment. The only question remaining for most people is what to do about it. Should we aggressively fight global warming, should we fight it piecemeal with gradual measures, or do we have time for more research?

Reasons for caution

How should the Christian evaluate this issue? We should first understand some of the assumptions and goals of not only those advocating we act now, but also the whole environmentalist movement. Second, we need to check the data—what we know for sure. Third, we will then be in a better position to evaluate any proposed courses of action to mitigate global warming.

Just like the creation/evolution issue, we need to separate raw data from interpretations. My theme verse in creation research is 1 Thessalonians 5:21: "But examine everything carefully; hold fast to that which is good" (NASB). We are to hold fast to the Bible as God's word and instruction book to us and to Jesus as our

Lord, Savior, and Creator. We should evaluate everything, and not at the superficial level. I examine the data, the assumptions, and the interpretations before I delve into biblical solutions to earth science problems.

Christians especially need to be cautious when it comes to the issue of global warming and other environmental issues. One of the reasons is that these issues have been hijacked by individuals who desire to change our way of life, and in particular, the Christian worldview that has guided the Western Hemisphere. Gene Edward Veith concluded: "A big part of the problem is that the current environmental movement has been hijacked by the far left."[6] There are also pantheists involved. These groups have agendas for social engineering. Second, some environmentalists are promulgating misinformation, as will be documented below. It is important that we examine what is known for sure before we speculate on future climate scenarios. Third, those who believe we must act now dominate public discussion and are served by a biased media. Fourth, computer simulations of climate are not always accurate predictors of the future and, with a doubling of carbon dioxide, exaggerate the amount of global warming. But too many people take these simulations as authoritative. Fifth, doomsayers use ad hominem arguments against those who disagree with them—a sign of a weak case and a refusal to enter into reasonable dialog.

Just recently, eighty-six prominent Christian leaders jumped on the doomsayer bandwagon with the Evangelical Climate Initiative (ECI).[7] Based on a report in *World* magazine, it looks like many of these evangelicals have not examined the subject in depth and were influenced by the barrage of propaganda.[8] The Evangelical Interfaith Stewardship Alliance has recently taken the ECI to task for poor analysis of the situation, and the likelihood that the poor would be harmed by draconian government regulations that attempt to curb carbon dioxide emissions. For example, government actions that curb greenhouse gases likely would cause the price of energy to jump astronomically. The poor could not afford energy that is required for development.

Examples of hysteria

Examples of misinformation and hysteria are not hard to find. One of the most recent examples of hysteria was a special report on global warming published in the April 3, 2006, issue of *Time* magazine.[9] The article flatly states without any qualifications, "The climate is crashing, and global warming is to blame."[10] Humans are blamed for global warming, and the potentially harmful effects are emphasized. The article claims that serious debate has quietly ended (although this is untrue) and lists many devastating weather, climate and environmental occurrences. Serious debate has only ended because radical environmentalists now dominate the discussion and malign those who disagree. This is not unlike the creation/evolution debate.

There are many other examples of wrong information, half-truths, and hysteria. In the January 22, 1996, issue of *Time* magazine, the front cover exclaimed, "The hot zone—blizzards, floods & hurricanes: blame global warming."[11] Believe it or not, even blizzards such as the powerful East Coast northeaster of January 1996 have been blamed on global warming by some advocates. It seems like some believe all bad weather is caused by global warming. One of the problems in countering such misinformation is that people have short memories or do not read weather history.

Probably the most outrageous example of false information is a video produced in 1990 that claimed world temperatures would rise 55°F (30°C) by the year 2050![12]

There is even a dramatic movie promoting an ice age rapidly caused by global warming.[13] Although the movie was admitted to be a Hollywood exaggeration, many scientists see such an ice age, caused by global warming, developing more slowly, perhaps over of the course of several decades. This belief has been reinforced by what are believed to be indications of abrupt climate change shown by ice cores from the Greenland Ice Sheet.[14] In the introduction to a special issue of the *Journal of Geophysical Research* on ice cores, Hammer and others stated:

"These millennial-scale events represent quite large climate deviations: probably 20°C in central Greenland . . . . The events often begin or end rapidly: changes equal to most of the glacial-interglacial differences commonly occur over decades, and some indicators, more sensitive to shifts in the pattern of atmospheric circulation, change in as little as 1–3 years."[15]

Such temperature changes in Greenland are related to the atmospheric circulation and would affect much of the Northern Hemisphere. Such rapid changes are indeed scary, but their deductions are based on their wrong interpretations of ice cores as a result of their assumption that the ice sheets are millions of years old.[16]

Al Gore wrote a book on global warming in which he seemed to believe every dire prediction of the radical environmentalists.[17] Recently, he has produced a video documentary with an accompanying book called *An Inconvenient Truth*. The video contains the same old misinformation. M. Bergen stated:

"But Mr. Gore's radical political agenda and tendency for half-truth have undergone no such makeover . . . Mr. Gore employs stage tricks, straw men, and well-rehearsed rhetoric to contend that opposition views on climate change are rooted in callous profiteering."[18]

Mr. Gore's hysterical and ad hominem attacks are typical of doomsayers. It is common for these advocates to claim that those who disagree with them are working for the oil companies. But we should look at the agendas of the radical environmentalists, and the great economic benefit for them to keep the pot stirred

The data

We should look at the observational data before we hypothesize about future climate scenarios. The probable average degree of surface warming in the Northern Hemisphere since 1880 has been only 1.2°F (0.7°C).[19] Figure 1 shows this warming. However, this number has resulted from the analysis of complex data. Over the years, measurement techniques of land and ship temperatures have changed. For terrestrial stations, the instrument shelters have changed locations, the type of thermometer has changed, the time of observation has changed and the microclimate around the shelter has changed. Man-made effects that are unrelated to increased greenhouse gases also can affect temperature readings over the years. The most notorious problem is the urban heat island effect, where the concrete of expanding cities heats up the air. Those who have analyzed the temperature record claim to have dealt with this problem, but some skeptics question whether researchers have excised all the urban heat island effect.[20]

So, it seems likely that global warming has occurred based on the temperature measurements, retreating glaciers, and other effects. However, doomsayers like to claim that skeptics do not believe in any global warming. This is untrue, since practically all skeptics agree that some global warming is occurring. This is not the issue. Patrick Michaels and Robert Balling, climatologists and critics of global warming hype, admit:

"In the broadest perspective, global warming is a very real thing, undeniable from surface temperature readings taken over much of the planet in the last 100 years."[21]

But there are also climatic effects other than carbon dioxide that have changed the temperature trends over the years. John Christy and Roy Spencer give an example of increased irrigation in the San Joaquin Valley causing warmer nighttime and cooler daytime temperatures, especially in summer.[22] Christy and Spencer conclude: "And I [Christy] always say that improvements still have to be made on a lot of our surface temperature data sets and that is what I spend a lot of my time doing."[23]

Christy and Spencer of the University of Alabama pioneered the use of satellites to measure the temperature of the troposphere. Their data had shown only a slight rise in temperature since 1979, compared to a substantial rise from the surface data during that period. Taking away the strong 1998 El Niño year, there was no significant change at all. However, scientists have recently found errors in the satellite data, although their analysis was in error itself.[24] Christy and Spencer went back and corrected their satellite data, and now it agrees within the lower end of the error bars of the surface data. Christy and Spencer sum up their satellite data: "So it is correct scientifically to say there is no significant discrepancy in the global temperatures between the surface and the satellite."[25]

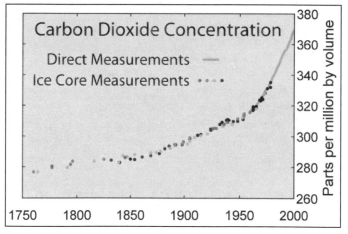

Figure 3. The carbon dioxide concentration in the atmosphere has increased over the last 250 years, based on both direct atmospheric measurements and sampling of gases trapped in ice cores. Source: Global Warming Art, globalwarmingart. com/wiki/Image:Carbon_History_and_Flux_Rev_png

Another key observation is that carbon dioxide has been increasing in the atmosphere since measurements were initiated in the late 1950s (Figure 3).[26] The level of carbon dioxide has likely been increasing since about 1850 due to the industrial revolution and the destruction of tropical rainforests. Other greenhouse gases have also been increasing. It is well known that carbon dioxide will enhance the greenhouse effect. But, it is also well known that carbon dioxide is a minor greenhouse gas and that water vapor is the primary greenhouse gas by far. Carbon dioxide provides less than 5% of the greenhouse warmth that makes our planet livable. It is the water vapor that actually stabilizes our climate.[27] If it gets too hot, evaporation will increase and clouds will cool the climate by reflecting sunlight from the tops of the white clouds. It also works the other way; cooler temperatures result in less cloudiness and more absorption of solar radiation at the surface.

That is the data, and both advocates and skeptics of runaway greenhouse warming start with this same data. The problem is over the interpretation of the data, just like in the creation/evolution controversy. There are three main interpretive problems: (1) how much of the warming is caused by man adding carbon dioxide to the atmosphere and how much is from natural fluctuations, (2) how much temperature increase is expected from increased carbon dioxide, and (3) will the harm from rising temperatures outweigh the benefit from warmer temperatures? I will analyze each of these interpretive aspects below. A related question is what can we do to minimize temperature change and how can we measure progress?

Natural versus man-made global warming?

There are indeed natural climatic fluctuations that cause warmer temperatures. A certain percentage of recent global warming is due to long-term natural fluctuations, including effects of the sun.[28] Volcanoes can also cause short-term cooling[29,30] but a lack of volcanism can result in warmer temperatures. From

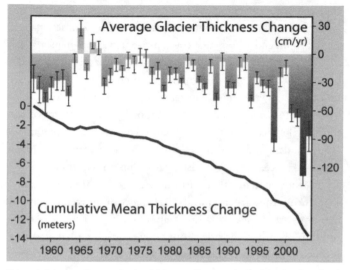

Figure 4. Average changes in the thickness of mountain glaciers, shown as both annual changes and the accumulated change since the late 1950s. Source: Global Warming Art, globalwarmingart.com/wiki/Image:Glacier_Mass_Balance_png

about 1400 to 1880, the Little Ice Age occurred,[31] in which practically all the glaciers in the world advanced, whereas now they are receding (Figure 4). At times people could ice skate on the Thames River in London, whereas that is unthinkable today. The Little Ice Age was likely caused by the combination of slightly less energy from the sun and more volcanism, both of which allow the surface of the earth to cool. There were periods during the Little Ice Age in which the sun exhibited few sunspots. Few sunspots cause a cooler solar temperature and less solar radiation because the stronger compensating effect of solar faculae is also reduced. Before the Little Ice Age, there was the Medieval Warm Period. So natural fluctuations in the past have been significant.[27]

Scientists are uncertain how much global warming is caused by these natural fluctuations. Roy Spencer stated:

"We need to find out how much of the warming we are seeing

could be due to mankind, because I still maintain we have no idea how much you can attribute to mankind. Jim Hansen had his smoking gun and said that he could prove that it's all man-made."[32]

Jim Hansen is a leading doomsayer, and these advocates tend to believe that all the global warming is caused by man. So the belief in how much warming is natural depends upon one's bias. Right now it is too soon to know the proportion. Beisner and others stated, "The mechanisms driving natural climate variations are too poorly understood to be included accurately in computer climate models. Hence, the models risk overstating human influences."[33]

Further evidence that natural fluctuations are significant is that during the early and mid-1970s, a cooling trend increased the amount of sea ice. This happened at a time when the buildup of carbon dioxide should have caused global warming. It initiated the idea that the ice age was around the corner, since according to the Milankovitch mechanism, the next ice age is due soon. Several books with this theme were published. One of them was *The Cooling: Has the Next Ice Age Already Begun? Can we Survive it?*[34] Climatologist Stephen Schneider published *The Genesis Strategy: Climate and Global Survival*, in which he asked, "Would a new cycle of droughts related to a global cooling trend portend chronic famine and world chaos?"[35] Yes, global cooling would initiate droughts. It is interesting that after the cooling trend petered out and global warming continued, Schneider dusted off the drought scare, but this time for global warming:

"What is more, several climate models predict that summer precipitation will actually decline in Midcontinental areas, including the central plains of the U.S. . . . . A decline in agricultural productivity in the Middle West and Great Plains, for example, could be disastrous for farmers and the U.S. economy."[36]

A significant proportion of the global warming has been an increase in nighttime and winter temperatures, which do not impact man and the environment as much as an increase during the day or summer. Although it was previously believed that the Arctic was not warming, it certainly seems to be warming today.[37] However, the South Pole seems to be cooling.[38]

So, for the time being and until more certain information is available, I will assume that half of the 1.2°F (0.7°C) rise is caused by natural long-term climatic cycles and the other half is due to man-made global warming. This means that the man-made temperature rise since the late 1880s is likely only about 0.6°F (0.3°C) or less.

How much warming after carbon dioxide doubles?

Climate specialists run computer simulations in order to determine the temperature sensitivity to increasing carbon dioxide. In the model, they double the amount of CO_2, leaving all other variables the same between computer runs, and see how much the temperature rises. There have been many climate models developed with many types of simulations with a wide variety of temperature responses. For a doubling of carbon dioxide, the simulations predict a temperature rise ranging from 3 to 11°F (1.5 to 6°C).[39] Figure 1 shows some of these temperature projections to the year 2100. Unfortunately, many environmentalists, politicians, and media celebrities take such imperfect climate simulations literally, which is problematic. No wonder we have a greenhouse scare.

But, let us look more closely at the data. The amount of CO_2 added to the atmosphere since 1880 is about 30%. Other greenhouse gases, such as methane, also have increased. In order to compare these other gases to CO_2, researchers put them into CO_2 equivalency units, which adds another 30% (see solid curve in Figure 3). So, essentially CO_2 has increased 60%. This 60% rise in CO_2 and its equivalency units has resulted in approximately a 0.6°F (0.3°C) rise in temperature. At this rate, a doubling of CO_2 will produce only a 1°F temperature rise. The climate simulations are, therefore, much too sensitive to the effects of CO_2. The super-sensitivity of the climate simulations could be due to the problems in estimating global variables in the models. Clouds, precipitation, and radiation are notoriously difficult to parameterize in the models.[40] Ocean processes and snow and ice reflectivities[41] are also not handled well by the models.

Doomsayers counter that the increase in pollution, mainly sulfur dioxide, causes a cooling effect, masking the effect of the warming.[42,43] Although there is probably some truth in this secondary hypothesis, Christy and Spencer maintain that it is speculation.[44]

Will there be a net harm to man and the environment?

Those who believe we must act now naturally emphasize the negative effects of global warming. But what about positive benefits? Will the positive benefits outweigh the negative benefits?

More people would be expected to die of the heat from global warming, advocates of a hot earth are quick to point out. But fewer people should die of the cold. Since nearly ten times the number of deaths result from severe cold than from severe heat,[45] global warming should save more lives. Furthermore, affordable energy, which gives off carbon dioxide, is needed to protect from extreme heat as well as extreme cold. More warmth will also result in an increased growing season and more area for agriculture.

Increased drought, of course, would be quite harmful to man. However, Christy and Spencer show that there has been no long-term increase in drought or wetness, although there is significant variability from year to year.[44] Some scientists claimed that droughts would increase in the future with further global warming, but this is speculative. Increasing temperature results in increasing water vapor in the air and increasing precipitation. Global precipitation increased 1% per decade during the twentieth century.[46] Thus, global warming means a wetter planet causing more plant growth, which should be a boon to agriculture. Besides, more plants will soak up some of the extra carbon dioxide, producing more growth and requiring less water.

More frequent and intense hurricanes obviously would be a great detriment to man and the environment. Warmer atmospheric temperatures result in warmer ocean temperatures, which fuel hurricanes. So, some increase in hurricanes should be expected, but the question is how much of an increase. Much discussion has ensued lately because of the four strong hurricanes that slammed into the southeast United States in 2005. Some researchers have made extraordinary claims on future hurricane deaths and damage.[46] The significant intensification of hurricanes and their frequency is controversial.[47,48] Christy and Spencer show a graph of hurricane strikes in the United States since 1850, not including 2005, that shows no significant trend.[49] The increase in deaths and damage is mainly because more people have built near the coast.

There is also no trend or maybe a downward trend in the frequency of strong tornadoes in Oklahoma.[50] The number of weak tornadoes has increased, but this is likely due to increased detection and reporting.

Then there are the negative effects if draconian government action is taken to curb the increase in carbon dioxide. Christy and Spencer say that the change in temperature from reduced carbon dioxide emissions likely would be unmeasureable,[25] while the cost to fight global warming would be well in excess of a trillion dollars per year.[51] The economic hardship, especially on the poor, would be substantially greater than any purported slowing of global warming.[52]

In regard to a rise in sea level, the magnitude of which is under dispute, people can slowly move inland or build more and higher dikes, since the climate change would be slow.[51] One interesting beneficial aspect to global warming would be increased shipping in the Arctic Ocean.[53]

So the jury is out on whether global warming will have a net harmful effect on man and the environment. What is needed is more objective research on the level of harm.

A new study of northward oceanic heat transport in the North Atlantic claims that the transport has already decreased 30%, based on 47 years of measurements.[3] Computer climate simulations had suggested that such a decrease would require a global temperature increase of 7 to 11°F (4–6°C) after nearly a century.[3] Some scientists are afraid of an abrupt climate change coming soon, and believe we need to act now. However, the reduced heat flow has caused no climatic effect in Europe. Moreover, Carl Wunsch of MIT believes the climatic significance of the heat transport is greatly overblown, emphasizing that it is difficult to stop the northward heat transport.[54] Wunsch further writes that there are many unknowns associated with ocean and atmospheric climatic interactions, and that climate simulations have many difficulties. Besides, the average wind drives the ocean currents and is the most important factor responsible for the northward heat transport. The addition of fresh water on the ocean surface will not slow the heat flow, as has been assumed in climate simulations.

More research needed

Clearly, more careful research is needed. All positions should have a say on the issue. Unfortunately, many qualified critics are demonized by the media and proponents of runaway global warming. Critics are commonly accused of believing in a flat earth.[27] Furthermore, we need to compare the potential benefits with the potential harms of global warming. Those evangelicals who signed the ECI need to study both sides of the issue (1 Thessalonians 5:21) instead of jumping on the doomsayer bandwagon. And if the evidence shows that global warming should be reduced, we should find and invest in new, cost-effective technologies that do so.[27]

1. T. Appenzeller, D.R. Dimick, D. Glick, F. Montaigne, and V. Morell, "The heat is on," *National Geographic* 206 no. 4 (2004): 2–75.

2. S. Milius, "Pumped-up poison ivy; carbon dioxide boosts plant's size, toxicity," *Science News* 169 no. 22 (2006): 339.

3. H.L. Bryden, H.R. Longworth, and S.A. Cunningham, "Slowing of the Atlantic meridional overturning circulation at 25°N," *Nature* 438 (2005): 655–657.

4. Oregon Petition Project, www.oism.org/pproject/s33p37.htm.

5. M.J. Oard, *The Weather Book* (Green Forest, AR: Master Books, 1997), pp. 70–71.

6. G.E. Veith, "To protect and conserve," *World* 21 no. 20 (2006): 30.

7. www.christiansandclimate.org. Also see March, 2006, *Christianity Today*, page 9.

8. M. Bergin, "Greener than Thou," *World* 21 no. 16 (2006): 18–21.

9. J. Kluger, "Global warming," *Time* 167 no. 14 (2006): 28–42.

10. Kluger, Ref. 9, p. 34.

11. Anonymous, "The hot zone," *Time* 127 no. 4 (1996): 20–23.

12. Anonymous, "The Fragile Planet: Alterations in the Atmosphere," *Films for the Humanities and Sciences*, Princeton, New Jersey, 1990.

13. M.J. Oard, "The greenhouse warming hype of the movie The Day After Tomorrow," *Acts and Facts Impact* #373, 2004, Institute for Creation Research, El Cajon, CA.

14. M.J. Oard, *The Frozen Record: Examining the Ice Core History of the Greenland and Antarctic Ice Sheets* (Santee, CA: Institute for Creation Research, 2005), pp. 123–132.

15. C.U. Hammer, P.A. Mayewski, D. Peel, and M. Stuiver, "Preface," *Journal of Geophysical Research* 102 no. C12 (1997): 6,315.

16. Oard, Ref. 14, pp. 1–199.

17. A. Gore, *Earth in the Balance: Ecology and the Human Spirit* (New York, NY: Houghton Mifflin Company, 1992).

18. M. Bergin, "Convenient spin," *World* 21 no. 24 (2006): 26

19. Kluger, Ref. 9, p. 38.

20. R.C. Balling, Jr., "Global warming: messy models, decent data, and pointless policy," in R. Bailery, ed., *The True State of the Planet* (New York, NY: The Free Press, 1995), pp. 83–107.

21. P.J. Michaels and R.C. Balling, Jr., *The Satanic Gases: Clearing the Air about Global Warming*, (Washington, DC: CATO Institute, 2000), p. 2.

22. J. Christy and R. Spencer, "Satellite temperature data," George C. Marshall Institute, 2006, pp. 11–14. www.marshall.org/pdf/materials/415.pdf

23. Christy and Spencer, Ref. 22, p. 15.

24. Christy and Spencer, Ref. 22, pp. 18–19.

25. Christy and Spencer, Ref. 22, p. 16.

26. C.D. Keeling, T.P. Whorf, M. Wahlen, and J. van der Plicht, "Interannual extremes in the rate of rise of atmospheric carbon dioxide since 1980," *Nature* 375 (1995): 666–670.

27. Christy and Spencer, Ref. 22, p. 27.

28. J. Lean, J. Beer, and R. Bradley, "Reconstruction of solar irradiance since 1610: Implications for climate change," *Geophysical Research Letters* 22 no. 23 (1995): 3,195–3,198.

29. M.J. Oard, *An ice Age Caused by the Genesis Flood*, (Santee, CA: Institute for Creation Research, 1990).

30. M.J. Oard, *Frozen In Time: The Woolly Mammoth, the Ice Age, and the Bible* (Green Forest, AR: Master Books, 2004), pp. 71–74.

31. B. Fagan, *The Little Ice Age: How climate Made History 1300–1850*, (New York, NY: Basic Books, 2000).

32. Christy and Spencer, Ref. 22, p. 28.

33. E.C. Beisner, P.K. Driessen, R. McKitrick, and R.W. Spencer, "A call to truth, prudence, and protection of the poor: An evangelical response to global warming," 2006, p. 10. www.interfaithstewardship.org/pdf/CalltoTruth.pdf

34. L. Ponte, *The Cooling: Has the Next Ice Age Already Begun? Can We Survive It?* (Englewood

Cliffs, NJ: Prentice-Hall, 1976).

35. S.H. Schneider, *The Genesis strategy: Climate and Global Survival*, (New York, NY: Plenum Press, 1976), p. x.

36. S.H. Schneider, "The Changing Climate," *Scientific American* 261 no. 3 (1989): 77.

37. N. Lubick, "Arctic amplification: the northern latitudes provide early warning for global climate change," *Geotimes* 51 no. 3 (2006): 30–33.

38. Christy and Spencer, Ref. 22, p. 19.

39. S.H. Schneider, "What is 'dangerous' climate change?" *Nature* 411 (2001): 17–19.

40. Christy and Spencer, Ref. 22, p. 30.

41. J. Hansen and L. Nazarenko, "Soot climate forcing via snow and ice albedos," *Proceedings of the National Academy of Science* 101 no. 2 (2004): 423–428.

42. Mitchell, J.F.B., T.C. Johns, J.M. Gregory, and S.F.B. Tett, "Climate response to increasing levels of greenhouse gases and sulphate aerosols," *Nature* 376 (1995): 501–504.

43. D. Rosenfeld, "Aerosols, clouds, and climate," *Science* 312 no. 1 (2006): 323–1,324.

44. Christy and Spencer, Ref 22, p. 20.

45. Beisner et al., Ref. 33, p. 6.

46. M.N. Evans, "The woods fill up with snow," *Nature* 440 no. 1 (2006): 120–1,121.

47. A. Witze, "Tempers flare at hurricane meeting," *Nature* 441 (2006): 11.

48. Witze, A., "Bad weather ahead," *Nature* 441 (2006): 564–566.

49. Christy and Spencer, Ref. 22, p. 21.

50. Christy and Spencer, Ref. 22, pp. 22–23.

51. Beisner et al., Ref. 33, p. 13.

52. Beisner et al., Ref. 33, pp. 1–24. Also see http://www.interfaithstewardship.org/pdf/OpenLetter.pdf.

53. Hansen and Nazarenko, Ref. 41, p. 424.

54. C. Wunsch, "Abrupt climate change: An alternative view," *Quaternary Research* 65 (2006): 191–203. E.W. Cliver, V. Boriakoff, and J. Feynman, "Solar Cariability and Climate Change: Geomagnetic AA Index and Global Surface Temperature," *Geophysical Research Letters* 25 no. 7 (1998): 1,035–1,038.

Michael J. Oard
National Weather Service (Ret.)
BS, Atmospheric Science, University of Washington, 1969
MS, Atmospheric Science, University of Washington, 1973

Mike has an MS in atmospheric science from the University of Washington and is now retired after working as a meteorologist with the US National Weather Service in Montana for 30 years. He is a prolific author, having written more than 40 technical papers and five books. His main area of interest and research is Noah's Flood and the Ice Age that followed.

How Much Global Warming Is Natural?

by Michael J. Oard

The concern over global warming seems to be escalating. We hear a steady media drumbeat that man has caused practically all the global warming, and we need to act now to avoid disaster. Al Gore seems to be the leader in all this hype with his movie and book, *An Inconvenient Truth*.[1] Although backing away from the sea level rise that is supposed to occur by 2100 (one foot),[2] the United-Nations-sponsored Intergovernmental Panel of Climate Change (IPCC) continued the drumbeat in its latest 2007 report. The most widely read scientific journals *Science* and *Nature* have an article on the effects and dangers of man-made global warming almost weekly. Outlandish statements are rampant, such as, "A well-known environmental spokesperson warns that future sea-level rise will drown much of creation."[3] A woman even aborted her baby, saying that she was reducing her "carbon footprint."[3,5]

All these voices assume that practically all the 1.2°F global warming since 1880 is caused by man, and only a tiny bit is natural. But other voices can be found in the recent literature that conclude that natural processes are significant, especially before 1980.[4,5,6,7,8,9,10,11] In fact, many researchers believe that natural process are predominant before 1980.

Natural solar irradiance

There are several natural processes that can affect global temperatures.

One of them is El Niño, a warming of the ocean water near the Pacific equator, which also causes global warming of the atmosphere. It is responsible for the anomalous warm year of 1998.

Then there are volcanic eruptions that spread sulfur aerosols (tiny particles about the size of a micron or less) into the stratosphere, which reflect some of the sunlight back to space, cooling the surface. Such aerosols slowly fall out of the stratosphere and have been observed to cool the earth up to about one degree Fahrenheit for a few years.

However, the most significant and long-lasting natural process is the change in total solar irradiance (TSI) from the sun. I was taught in atmospheric science classes in college that the sunlight is never changing. In fact, the amount of sunshine at the top of the atmosphere was called the "solar constant." However, ever since satellites have been measuring solar radiation since 1978, we now realize that the sunshine isn't constant. It changes by a slight amount due to sunspots and faculae that change with time on the sun's surface. Sunspots are dark, cool spots, while faculae are bright, hot spots—they usually occur together.[12] The net effect is that when there are many cooler sunspots, the hot faculae more than make up for the cool spots. Thus, there is more solar radiation when there are more sunspots.

Sunspots run in cycles. There is the familiar 11-year cycle. Then there is a 22-year cycle, and there is a long period, chaotic cycle that lasts several hundred years. During the Little Ice Age that lasted from about 1300 to 1880, sunspots were at a general minimum, suggesting that effects on the sun caused the Little Ice Age. During this time, practically all the glaciers in the world advanced, and unusual cold spawned a number of disasters. In fact, there were three periods during the Little Ice Age when the number of sunspots was quite small compared to the average. One of those is the Maunder Minimum, between 1645 to 1715, in which about 50 sunspots were detected during the entire

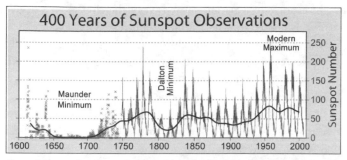

400 Years of Sunspot Observations

Figure 5. The sun has shown considerable variability, including the long Maunder Minimum when almost no sunspots were observed, the less severe Dalton Minimum, and increased sunspot activity during the last fifty years, known as the Modern Maximum. Source: Global Warming Art, www.globalwarmingart.com/wiki/Image:Sunspot_Numbers_png

period, while normally there should be 40,000 to 50,000 spots.[13] This was one of the coldest periods of the Little Ice Age (Figure 5).

Before the Little Ice Age, there was the Medieval Warm Period between about 900 and 1300. This was the time when the Vikings colonized southwest Greenland, and records indicate that good wine grapes were grown in southern England. Since sunspots have been detected only since 1610, the evidence for the Medieval Warm Period relies on carbon-14 in tree rings and beryllium-10 in ice cores. These proxies, as they are called, which are generally good for the past one or two thousand years,[14] indicate that sunspot activity was very high during the Medieval Warm Period.[15,16] This warm period has sometimes been denied or minimized by advocates of man-made global warming. So, if the sun can cause the dramatic effects of the Medieval Warm Period and the Little Ice Age, when carbon dioxide was in steady state, then why can't the sun be causing a significant amount of global warming since the Little Ice Age?

More recent statistical analysis

One of the main reasons why alarmists have minimized the effects of the sun on climate is because the mechanism of how slight changes in TSI can warm or cool the climate by a degree or two is poorly known.17 One promising recent hypothesis is that when the number of sunspots is low, the sun's magnetic field is weaker, causing more cosmic rays to impinge on the earth.18 More cosmic rays may cause more clotudiness, which reflects more sunlight back to space cooling the earth's surface.

Because of controversial hypotheses linking the sun to climate, researchers have had to resort to statistical comparisons. Scafetta and West have led this research over the past several years, showing statistically that the changes in TSI on the sun are significantly correlated to global warming since 1900 and even before.[17] Because global warming increased significantly from 1910 to about 1950, proportional to the TSI, while carbon dioxide increased only a little, Scafetta and West attribute 76% of the warming to natural causes on the sun![18] Then there was a cooling period in the 1950s to 1970s, again proportional to TSI, but totally missed by increasing carbon dioxide. Some readers may remember the books and magazine articles that came out in the 1970s predicting the next ice age was due soon.

The period from 1980 to the present is questionable and controversial as to how much of the strong rise in global warming was natural and how much was manmade. Scafetta and West believe that only 25 to 35% of this warming is due to natural causes while the rest is manmade.[18] However, even this percentage is controversial because there is more than one estimate of TSI. Scafetta and West use a compromise TSI between a reconstruction that shows only a small change and one that shows a large change in TSI since 1980. Alarmists seem to focus on the one that shows the small change. For the twentieth century, Scafetta and West estimate natural causes from the sun contributed 45 to 50% to the global warming.

Scafetta and West have recently updated their figures and reported an even stronger correlation between global warming and natural changes in sunlight.[19] They show that monthly global average temperatures correlate to the 11-year, 22-year, and longer-term TSI cycle. Because sunspots are relatively low at present in the 11-year cycle, the decreased sunlight is correlated to cooler temperatures since 2002: "In particular, since 2002 the temperature data present a global cooling, not a warming!"[20]

They conclude: "The non-equilibrium thermodynamic models we used suggest that the Sun is influencing climate significantly more than the IPCC report claims. If climate is as sensitive to solar changes as the above phenomenological [statistical] findings suggest, the current anthropogenic [man-made] contribution to global warming is significantly overestimated. We estimate that the Sun could account for as much as 69% of the increase in earth's average temperature, depending on the TSI reconstruction used."[20]

The reason that climate models and the IPCC have not picked up on the strong influence of the sun on temperatures is because present-day climate models dismiss the variability in monthly average global temperature as climate noise, and hence ignore it. They also use the TSI that shows the lowest amount of solar irradiance since 1980.

Natural processes are obviously affecting the surface temperature. I will stick with my previous estimate of 50% natural and 50% manmade,[21] since the figure of 69% ever since about 1900 used by Scafetta and West is for a medium to high TSI estimate for the past 25 to 30 years. If the low TSI is correct (Scafetta and West think not) and man-made global warming has dominated during the past 25 to 30 years, the century average would be around 50%, since natural processes on the sun dominated before 1980.

What does it all mean?

What this means is that manmade global warming is only about 0.6°F, while the sun contributed another 0.6°F. Man's contribution is slight, and not enough man-made warming has occurred to panic over. There is a good chance that man can do nothing or only very little to change the manmade portion, even if he spent what alarmists suggest to "fight" global warming (although we should always have been and should continue to be good stewards of the resources God has provided us). We have plenty of time for research.[22] We can also learn to adapt by making changes, if global warming continues its slow upward trend, such as building dikes for rising sea level. (Some scientists are actually predicting global cooling in the future based on trends on the sun, but this remains to be seen.) Spending hundreds of billions of dollars a year to "fight" global warming just doesn't make sense, and is more likely to ruin the economies of first-world nations than make any significant impact.

1. A. Gore, *An Inconvenient Truth: The Planetary Emergency of Global Warming and What We Can Do About It* (New York, NY: Rodale, 2006).
2. B. Lomborg, *Cool It: The Skeptical Environmentalists Guide to Global Warming* (New York, NY: Alfred A. Knopf, 2007), pp. 60–72.
3. Ruddiman, W., "Act now (but how?)," *Science* 319 (2008): 285.
4. T.J. Crowley, and K.Y. Kim, "Comparison of Proxy Records of Climate Change and Solar Forcing," *Geophysical Research Letters* 23 no. 4 (1996): 359–362.
5. E.W. Cliver, V. Boriakoff, and J. Feynman, "Solar Cariability and Climate Change: Geomagnetic AA Index and Global Surface Temperature," *Geophysical Research Letters* 25 no. 7 (1998): 1,035–1,038.
6. P. Foukal, "A Comparison of Variable Solar Total and Ultraviolet Irradiance Outputs in the 20th Century," *Geophysical Research Letters* 29 no. 23 (2002): 1–4.
7. C.M. Ammann, G.A. Meehl, W.M. Washington, and C.S. Zender, "A Monthly and Latitudinally Varying Volcanic Forcing Dataset in Simulations of 20th Century Climate," *Geophysical Research Letters* 30 no. 12 (2003): 1–4.
8. G.A. Meehl, W.M. Washington, C.M. Amman, J.M. Arblaster, T.M.L. Wigley, and C. Tebaldi, "Combinations of Natural and Anthropogenic Forcings in Twentieth-Century Climate," *Journal of Climate* 17 no. 3 (2004): 721–3, 727. N. Scaffetta and B.J. West, "Estimated Solar Contribution to the Global Surface Warming Using the ACRIM TSI Satellite Composite," *Geophysical Research Letters* 32, L18713 (2005): 1–4.
9. I.G. Usoskin, M. Schüssler, S.K. Solanki, and K. Mursula, "Solar Activity, Cosmic Rays, and Earth's Temperature: A Millennium-Scale Comparison," *Journal of Geophysical Research* 110, A10102 (2005): 1–10.
10. V. Courtillot, Y. Gallet, J.L. Le Mouël, F. Fluteau, and A. Genevey, "Are There Connections Between the Earth's Magnetic Field and Climate?" *Earth and Planetary Science Letters* 253 (2007): 328–339.
11. J. Lean, "Living with a Variable Sun," *Physics Today* 58 no. 6 (2005): 32-38.
12. RIAN, "Scientist Says Earth Could Soon Face New Ice Age," *Spero News*, www.speroforum.com.
13. M.J. Oard, *The Frozen Record: Examining the Ice Core History of the Greenland and Antarctic Ice Sheets* (Dallas, TX: Institute for Creation Research, 2005).
14. C. Loehle, "A 2000-Year Global Temperature Reconstruction Based on Non-tree Ring Proxies," *Energy and Environment* 18 nos. 7 & 8 (2007): 1,049–1,058.
15. C. Loehle and J.H. McCulloch, "Correction To: A 2000-Year Global Temperature Reconstruction Based on Non-tree Ring Proxies," *Energy and Environment* 19 no. 1 (2008): 93–100.

16. N. Scafetta, and B.J. West, "Phenomenological Reconstructions of the Solar Signature in the Northern Hemisphere Surface Temperature Records Since 1600," *Journal of Geophysical Research* 112, D24S03 (2007): 1–10.
17. J. Pasotti, "Daggers Are Drawn over Revived Cosmic Ray-Climate Link," *Science* 319 (2008): 144.
18. N. Scafetta and B.J. West, "Phenomenological Solar Contribution to the 1900–2000 Global Surface Warming," *Geophysical Research Letters* 33, L05708 (2006): 1–4.
19. N. Scafetta and B.J. West, "Is Climate Sensitive to Solar Variability?" *Physics Today* 61 no. 3 (2008): 50–51.
20. Scafetta and West, Ref. 19, p. 51.
21. M.J. Oard, "Human-Caused Global Warming Slight So Far," JOBSS, Answers in Genesis website: www.answersingenesis.org/articles/am/v1/n2/human-caused-global-warming.
22. M.J. Oard, "Global Warming," *Answers*, October–December 2006, pp. 24–26. www.answersingenesis.org/articles/am/v1/n2/global-warming

For biography of Michael J. Oard, see page 43.

Evidence for Global Warming

by Larry Vardiman

*T*he global warming issue will not go away. Evidence continues to mount that some type of warming is occurring, maybe temporarily or of longer duration. But, is it caused by man and can anything be done about it? Environmental activism to reduce carbon dioxide emissions has reached a new intensity. The U.S. Supreme Court is being asked to rule on a suit, which demands that the Environmental Protection Agency regulate the release of carbon dioxide as part of its air pollution responsibility. The president is being heavily lobbied to subscribe to the Kyoto Protocol which would require the U.S. to emit less carbon dioxide than it released in 1990.

A book and a movie with the titles, *An Inconvenient Truth,* which press the case for global warming were released during 2006 by Al Gore, former vice president of the United States.[1,2] He makes the case that man's actions in burning fossil fuels are projected to increase the concentration of carbon dioxide in the atmosphere to the highest levels in history. He insists that uncontrolled releases of carbon dioxide will eventually melt the polar caps completely, raising sea level and inundating many coastal communities like New York, Miami, New Orleans, and Los Angeles; and drastically changing agricultural patterns because of redistribution of temperature and precipitation.

And finally, on February 2, 2007, the Fourth IPCC Assessment Report on global warming was released. Interestingly, the report reduced the alarmist rhetoric because climate modelers found that they had overestimated the rise in global temperature and observations did not support the predictions.

Measures of global warming

For many years I have been a skeptic of global warming because the climate record available to assess the effects of increased carbon dioxide emission has been too short to say with confidence that the effect is real. There is no question that the concentration of carbon dioxide shown in Figure 1 has been increasing exponentially for almost 50 years now. These data were collected by C. C. Keeling of the Scripps Institute of Oceanography at the Mauna Loa Observatory, Hawaii.[3]

However, it is still unclear if the conclusions are valid that this increase in carbon dioxide is due to man's burning of fossil fuels and that it is causing the apparent recent warming trend which is melting the polar caps. Several questions continue to nag researchers in the climate community. Is the globe really warming? Are the polar caps really melting? How much of the increase in carbon dioxide is due to man's influence? If man were to attempt to reduce carbon dioxide emissions would it actually do any good? And finally, are there any other possible explanations for the apparent global warming? These are not simple questions and it will require a much longer period of record to be confident in any conclusions.

In order to answer the first two questions, massive amounts of global data must be averaged over a relatively long period of time. And because the effects of global warming are so small compared to the global average, great care must be taken to avoid bias in collection and analysis of the data. Many pitfalls in this process have already occurred which have produced a lack of confidence in the results.

I determined to take another look at the evidence and see if

I could detect any recent trends in the atmosphere, ocean, and cryosphere which would seem to support the concept of global warming, choosing to select several small data sets. The data sets I used are limited in spatial and temporal scope making them relatively easy to analyze without bias. However, the results need to be qualified because they don't necessarily reflect long-term, global trends.

The three data sets I analyzed were (1) the sea-surface temperature in the Gulf of Alaska,[4] (2) the frequency of hurricanes in the southeastern Atlantic and Caribbean,[5] and (3) the polar extent of sea ice in the Arctic Ocean.[6]

Analysis

If global warming is occurring then sea-surface temperature should also be increasing, hurricane frequency should be on the rise, and polar sea ice should be melting. Figures 2-4 show that the trends for all three processes seem to be consistent for at least the short term. Sea-surface temperature in the Gulf of Alaska has increased about 3% over the past 30 years. Hurricane frequency in the western Atlantic appears to have increased about 3% over the past 150 years. And, the Arctic sea-ice extent has decreased about 5% over the past 25 years. Note, within the general trends, however, shorter period oscillations occur. Hurricane frequency is the most variable, with 30–40 year periods of lower and higher frequency. This has become particularly noticeable since about 1995 when a sudden increase in the frequency of hurricanes hitting the southeastern U.S. followed a 30-year period of lower hurricane frequency. These shorter period oscillations are normal in most geophysical phenomena and are evident in the sea-surface temperature and Arctic sea-ice extent as well, although with less fluctuation.

Based on these limited observations, it appears likely that global warming seems to be occurring over at least the past 30–50 years. I would be quick to add, however, that because of the limited spatial coverage and short time period of these data, it is still not possible to say if these trends will continue. There may be even longer-period fluctuations which we don't yet see in the data. When long-period records of data are plotted, oscillations for many periods are often seen.

These data do not address the question about man's part in causing the warming trend. It is true that increased carbon dioxide concentration in the atmosphere would be expected to increase the greenhouse effect and possibly cause warming. It is unclear whether global warming is due to increased carbon dioxide concentration or if carbon dioxide concentration is the result of global warming. The oceans contain thousands of times more carbon dioxide than the atmosphere and can release significant quantities of carbon dioxide if they are warmed or the pH altered. If some, as yet, undiscovered process is warming the ocean, it could initiate the release of carbon dioxide from the ocean to the atmosphere which, in turn, is warmed even more by radiational heating.

One possible scenario may be found in a recent series of articles by Henrik Svensmark and Nigel Marsh, cosmic ray specialists from Denmark, who have shown an indirect connection between galactic cosmic ray (GCR) intensity and global temperature.[7,8,9] They are studying the influence of the Sun on the flow of GCR to earth. The Sun's changing sunspot activity influences the magnetosphere surrounding the earth permitting more GCR to strike the earth during high periods of activity. When the Sun is active, the intensity of GCR striking the earth is increased, causing more ionization in the atmosphere, creating more carbon-14, and possibly creating more cloud condensation nuclei (CCN). This increase in CCN, in turn, appears to create more low-level clouds which cool the earth. When the Sun is quiet the GCR intensity striking the earth is reduced, allowing the earth to warm. Svensmark and Marsh have shown a striking statistical correlation between sunspot activity and global cooling and warming over the past 1,000 years. The recent rise in global temperature may partially be due to current low solar activity supplemented by a recent increase in carbon dioxide concentration measured at Mauna Loa. The connection which still needs further study is the production of CCN and clouds by GCR.

Conclusions and recommendations

So, what can we conclude? I believe it is safe to say that:

Global warming appears to have been occurring for the last 30–50 years.

This warming may only be a short-term fluctuation but could be a longer-term trend.

Evidence is still inconclusive whether man is causing the warming.

No "natural" causes for global warming have been confirmed.

One possible new theory is that galactic cosmic radiation (GCR) modulated by solar activity affects low-level cloud cover and is causing the warming.

Global warming may affect some parts of our society negatively but would likely benefit others. In fact, the current warming trend may be returning our global climate closer to that prevalent in the Garden of Eden. Compared to climate changes which have occurred in earth history, a temperature rise of a few degrees is a small fluctuation which will not lead to a complete melting of the polar caps or another ice age. Earth has a stable environmental system with many built-in feedback systems to maintain a uniform climate. It was designed by God and has only been dramatically upset by catastrophic events like the Genesis Flood. Catastrophic climate change will occur again in the future, but only by God's intervention in a sudden, violent conflagration of planet earth in the end times (2 Peter 3:1–12).

1. A. Gore, *An inconvenient truth: The planetary emergence of global warming and what we can do about it,* (Emmaus, PA: Rodale Press, 2006).

2. A. Gore, *An inconvenient truth* (Paramount Classics, 2006).

3. C.D. Keeling et al., Carbon Dioxide Research Group, Scripps Institution of Oceanography (SIO), University of California, La Jolla, CA, 2004. http://cdiac.esd.ornl.gov/ftp/maunaloa-co2/maunaloa.co2.

4. NOAA National Data Buoy Center, 2006. Buoy #46001, Kodiak, AL. http://www.nodc.noaa.gov/BUOY/46001.html.

5. Best Track data documentation tape from the National Hurricane Center, 2006. http://weather.unisys.com/hurricane/atlantic/index.html.

6. Nimbus-7 satellite SMMR files of NASA Goddard Space Flight Center, 2006.

7. H. Svensmark, "Cosmic rays and Earth's climate," *Space Science Reviews* 93 (2000): 155–166.

8. N. Marsh and H. Svensmark, "GCR and ENSO trends in ISCCP-D2 low cloud properties," *Journal of Geophysical Research* 108 no. D6 (2003): 1–11.

9. N. Marsh and H. Svensmark, "Solar influence on Earth's climate," *Space Science Reviews* 107 (2003): 317–325.

Larry Vardiman
Astro-geophysics
Institute for Creation Research
PhD, Atmospheric Science, Colorado State University, 1974
MS, Atmospheric Science, Colorado State University, 1972
BS, Meteorology, St. Louis University, 1967
BS, Physics, University of Missouri, 1965

Dr. Larry Vardiman is a member of the American Meteorological Society and has authored numerous technical papers and books including overseeing the editing of the book, *Radioisotopes and the Age of the Earth*. Many of Dr. Vardiman's scientific contributions have been in the areas of cloud seeding, ice crystal growth and evolution, the age of the earth's atmosphere, ice sheet formation during the Ice Age, and catastrophic hurricane formation.

DVD Transcript

The following is a word-for-word transcript from the 48-minute documentary, Global Warming—A scientific and biblical exposé of climate change. *For biographical information about the experts featured in the DVD, see pages 86–92.*

INTRODUCTION

DR. JAY WILE: We have to figure out what's going on first.

DR. JOHN CHRISTY: Icebergs falling off and drought and deaths of thousands of animals.

Dr. RICHARD LAND: It is a doomsday scenario that there's absolutely no scientific evidence for.

DR. TIMOTHY BALL: To push to lower CO_2 levels, is in fact endangering the planet and life on it, much more than any increase in CO_2.

DR. E. CALVIN BEISNER: From the typical environmentalist prospective the best environment is nature untouched by human hands. That's not a biblical understanding at all.

DR. JAY WILE: It's not enough simply to listen to the propaganda and believe it. We have to actually reason through it.

ANNOUNCER: Coral Ridge Ministries and Answers in Genesis present "Global Warming—A Scientific and Biblical Exposé of Climate Change."

DR. JOHN CHRISTY: Global warming is a popular phenomenon now because of the expressions of disaster that tend to come along with the story. You can show a story that has big icebergs falling off and drought and deaths of thousands of animals and so on.

Well, that's going to get the media's attention, certainly people's attention.

NARRATOR: But with all the doomsday scenarios, what do scientists really know about global warming?

DR. JOHN CHRISTY: The simple answer on what is global warming is to say that the earth's temperature has risen in the past 150 years. We've been able to measure that with thermometers.

DR. ROY SPENCER: There isn't anybody I know that doesn't agree that we are unusually warm right now.

NARRATOR: But that's where the agreement among scientists ends.

DR. JOHN CHRISTY: Once you understand that the temperature is rising, the question is, "Well, why?" And that is where a number of issues come to bear and opinions because we cannot know for certain.

THE CAUSE

DR. JASON LISLE: At this point, I think the research is too preliminarily for us to say definitively what is causing global warming even though I think it is fairly well established that it's happening.

DR. LARRY VARDIMAN: Many of the measurements we have today with satellite and with surface temperature data on the ocean, these are only 30 years old. Even the measurements of carbon dioxide in the atmosphere, direct measurements only go up to 1958. So that's why it's only been just in the last few years that we've been able to get direct measurements that lead us to have more confidence there has been some change in temperature in the atmosphere.

GEORGE H. TAYLOR: As land use changes, climate changes, too. If you build a city, the temperatures tend to go up. And so in a lot of places it looks like we're seeing global warming in the urban areas and yet in rural areas there's not much at all. So this has been a big problem. But with the satellites measuring temperatures above the earth's surface, it's really getting an unbiased (unfettered by land use change) temperature trend. And now we have about 30 years of data and it is very interesting and very valuable data.

NARRATOR: The most widely publicized theory and the view presented in Al Gore's Oscar winning documentary, "An Inconvenient Truth," is that greenhouse gases are largely to blame for the warming.

DR. JOHN CHRISTY: Greenhouse gases are gases that absorb energy in a certain part of the spectrum that keeps thermal, or heat, energy in the atmosphere. I think the simplest way to think about this is that if you were in a desert at night, you find that it gets very cold. If you're in the southeastern United States at night, say Florida or Alabama, or somewhere, you'll find that the nighttime temperatures in the summer stay warm. Well, water vapor or humidity in the southeast is a greenhouse gas that keeps the heat in and doesn't allow it to escape at night.

DR. ROY SPENCER: Sunlight comes in, warms the earth. But what most people don't realize is that for all that sunlight coming in there has to be an equal amount of infrared heat energy going back out to outer space. Now the climate modelers claim that there's this fragile balance between the incoming sunlight and the outgoing infrared, and that when we add the CO_2 we're upsetting that delicate balance.

NARRATOR: CO_2, or carbon dioxide, is the greenhouse gas that grabs most of the headlines.

DR. ROY SPENCER: They make it sound like it's that radiation balance that determines what the temperature of the earth is. But I think that's the wrong way to look at. I think that it's the sunlight coming in that determines how warm things are going to get. Weather creates a greenhouse effect, which is mostly water vapor and clouds. And, in other words, the weather has control over the greenhouse effect, and if we add CO_2, I think the weather is going to change slightly in order to reduce the warming from that extra CO_2.

GEORGE H. TAYLOR: Some people say that CO_2 has a dominant effect on the earth's climate. And the models tend to make you believe that because they leave out all the other variables that I think really matter.

DR. JAY WILE: We have to figure out what's going on first. If it were as simple as excess carbon dioxide in the atmosphere (which we know is real) is causing the earth to warm up, then the data would support that. It doesn't.

DR. E. CALVIN BEISNER: The great question is, "How much, if at all, does that account for the warming that we have seen in recent years?" And the best scientific evidence that I see indicates that it is a very tiny proportion of the total cause, if in fact it can even be viewed as a part of the cause at all.

DR. LARRY VARDIMAN: The oceans contain much more carbon dioxide than the atmosphere does and if the temperature, the warming, occurs, and it warms the ocean, it releases carbon dioxide very much like a bottle of soda pop. When it's warm, it fizzes very easily. So the ocean will release carbon dioxide when it's warmer. That in turn explains the increases in carbon dioxide with the increase temperature but the temperature leads the carbon dioxide change.

DR. JOHN CHRISTY: We can't look out and develop an instrument that says, "This tells me why the temperature is changing." Some people think all that you see in terms of global warming is caused by humans and the greenhouse gases we emit because of energy production. Others say it's completely naturally induced like changes in the solar input from the sun or various ways in which the weather fluctuates due to natural changes in the ocean circulation or wind systems and so on like that.

NARRATOR: The bottom line is that contrary to popular reports, not all scientists agree that global warming is manmade.

DR. ROY SPENCER: I would say that the mainstream view of global warming is, "Yes, we are unusually warm right now and most of it is probably due to mankind." Now, you'll hear that there's a consensus of scientists that believe this. It turns out that there are very few scientists in the world that know enough about the whole problem to actually be able to cast judgment on this. So that if you hear that a thousand scientists agree that global warming is due to mankind, chances are only ten of that thousand actually know enough about the problem to cast any judgment on the issue at all.

DR. JASON LISLE: We don't really know for certain what's causing global warming. We know that it's happening, there is evidence to suggest that the earth's temperature has gone up a bit and there are many mechanisms that have been proposed. And of course, the one that I'm most interested in, as an astronomer, would be the astronomical aspects of that—namely the influence of the sun. We do know that the sun's overall intensity is greater when there are more sunspots. That's something that's been measured so that's definitive, but we don't know for certain if that's what's causing the increased temperatures on earth.

MICHAEL J. OARD: Al Gore says, in his "Inconvenient Truth," that there's consensus and other scientists in the media say there's a consensus but they're getting this from the United Nations Intergovernmental Panel on Climate Change—IPCC is the acronym for it. And they claim that there's a consensus of 2,500 scientists that now man is causing more most, if not all, the global warming. That's the claim consensus. But there isn't a consensus because there's a lot of meteorologists and atmospheric scientists and environmentalists that say that we believe that natural processes are a significant part of the global warming.

THE EFFECTS

NARRATOR: Aside from the causes of warming, the effects of global warming are also up for debate.

DR. ROY SPENCER: As far as Al Gore's movie goes, "An Inconvenient Truth," I think there was a lot of misrepresentation and half-truths in that movie. He showed a lot of dramatic footage of different things going on, you know, ice crashing off of glaciers into the ocean, and droughts, and floods. And of course, what he didn't mention was everything he showed in the movie happens naturally.

DR. LARRY VARDIMAN: The concern that many scientists have is that whether you have an ice age or whether you have warming, major warming, it's going to cause droughts, and doom and gloom. But there are benefits. For example, in the northern parts of the United States and in Canada if you have global warming you're going to have longer growing seasons up there and people will be able to live up there. It will be warmer to the south and there may be some places of drought but we have droughts today, so it's not a major effect.

DR. JASON LISLE: A lot of people when they hear about global warming, they have this doom and gloom mentality that it's just going to be a disaster and wipe out all life on earth. And really we need to consider that actually global warming may have a number of positive benefits as well. And now, certainly it will have some negative consequences but we need to consider the fact that, for example, human lives will probably be saved as a result of global warming because after all, more people die of exposure to cold than they do exposure to heat; and therefore, increasing earth's temperatures will likely result in fewer human causalities. Now that's something that people need to consider, as well as certain areas of the world becoming more habitable as a result of global warming, and granted, certain areas becoming less habitable as well. So things are going to change but that not all of it is negative change; and therefore, we ought to have a balanced view of global warming and not just have a reactionary position on it.

DR. JOHN CHRISTY: You know, in science, as Lord Kelvin said, all science is numbers. And so when I hear people talk about polar bears, I say, "Well, let's be scientific about them, let's count the polar bears." And it turns out the polar bear population has grown by a factor of over three in the last 40 years.

NARRATOR: Some experts say the record setting 2005 hurricane season is evidence for global warming, but not all agree.

DR. ROY SPENCER: There's a lot of uncertainty about whether hurricanes are either more frequent or more intense. Certainly, 2005 was a record year for hurricane hits in the United States. That was pretty amazing, but then you remember 2006 was a flop basically; it was below normal. And it turns out that since we only have good hurricane data, as far as how many hurricanes are out there in the Atlantic, since we've had weather satellites back in the 1970s, that we really don't know how many there were before then with much confidence.

DR. LARRY VARDIMAN: In the period from about 1970 to about 1995, there was a period of low hurricane frequency and we kind of got lulled into the period or lulled into the idea there wasn't going to be very many hurricanes. Suddenly, in the late 1990s and the early 2000s, we got a lot more hurricanes and they were more intense. Much of the damage, however, that was produced by these wasn't due to more hurricanes and more intense ones; it had to do more with the fact that we had more structures built along coastlines. There was more buildings, and more families, and more casinos. And when a hurricane hits one of those it's going to do a lot of damage.

NARRATOR: But what about the future? News reports claim global warming is the number one threat to our future survival as a planet, saying that ice caps could melt, submerging entire cities under the ocean.

DR. E. CALVIN BEISNER: For example, on sea level rise, people have—particularly because of Al Gore's movie, "An Inconvenient Truth"—they have these pictures in mind of sea level rising twenty, forty, sixty feet, something like that. Well, the Intergovernmental Panel on Climate Change estimates sea level rise through the entire 21st century at probably not more than a total of sixteen inches for the entire century.

DR. RICHARD LAND: Whether the oceans are going to rise two and a half feet over the next hundred years, whether they're going to rise twenty feet, which is the model that Al Gore uses for his "Inconvenient Truth," his crock-umentary that won an Oscar. I mean it is a doomsday scenario that there's absolutely no scientific evidence for; no reputable scientist is talking about a twenty foot increase in the oceans.

MICHAEL J. OARD: The amount of sea level rise has been downgraded over time. In the 1980s, they were talking about six feet of rise by 2100, and then it went down to two feet, and the latest 2007 IPCC report only said about one foot to maybe sixteen inches. And it's interesting, that estimated drop in sea level caused a lot of environmentalists to complain to the IPCC to not do that, not de-emphasize the sea level rise.

WHAT TO DO ABOUT IT

NARRATOR: Some experts say we should take aggressive action to reduce consumption of fossil fuels, not only to

protect the environment itself but also to save people living in poverty. Others say the opposite is true.

DR. ROY SPENCER: We have at least one million Africans dying each year because of a lack of access to electricity. We have Africans dying by the hundreds of thousands, mostly children, because we've got poor people burning wood and dung in huts, which cause respiratory illnesses, which kill mostly children. Meanwhile, these people can't have electricity because environmentalists, that don't even live in Africa, put pressure on their governments and don't let them build hydroelectric dams that could give them electricity and save their lives. So basically, what's happening is we are sacrificing the poor at the altar of radical environmentalism.

NARRATOR: Even if scientists don't have all the answers, Christians should be concerned about global warming, but they should also be concerned about their approach to the issue.

DR. E. CALVIN BEISNER: I think there are some very significant risks to evangelicals getting involved with this without really knowing the science or the economics well. The first and most important risk, the one that I care about the most, is that they might unwittingly endorse a policy that is very destructive to the poorest people in this world, the most vulnerable people. Those people desperately need abundant and cheap energy to drive the economic development that will lift them out of absolute poverty.

DR. RICHARD LAND: In Genesis chapter 2, Adam was put into the Garden to keep it and to till it. To keep it means to guard it and to protect it. To till it means to cause it to bring forth its fruit to develop it. For what purpose? For human good.

DR. ROY SPENCER: From a biblical standpoint, I think we are called to be good stewards of the environment. Right? And that's where Christians, you know, understandably get involved in environmentalism. Of course, what does "good stewardship" mean? I mean, it's clear that humans come first. But at the same time we shouldn't be destroying the environment wantonly. So there's a gray area, and people have to decide, you know, how far you go to protect the environment.

DR. RICHARD LAND: I think we need to, in our evangelical Christian churches, do a far better job than we have of helping people to understand what a biblical earth-keeping ethic is. What creation-care really means and what our responsibilities are in terms of creation-care and part of that being to understand that human beings come first in God's creation, not last, and are not irrelevant, and are not considered the enemies of God's creation.

A MAJOR THREAT?

MICHAEL J. OARD: The amount of global warming so far, since 1880 (the end of the Little Ice Age), is only 1.2 degrees Fahrenheit. 1.2 degrees Fahrenheit—that is not a lot to panic over. And I believe a good proportion of that could be, is from natural processes and it can be demonstrated from the literature.

DR. TIMOTHY BALL: CO_2 is presented as a pollutant because you want to show that it's the by-product of industry, which is what they're attacking. In fact, there is no life on earth without CO_2 in the atmosphere. Plants need it to produce oxygen and without that oxygen there is no living things on the planet. And to push to lower CO_2 levels is, in fact, endangering the planet and life on it much more than any increase in CO_2.

DR. LARRY VARDIMAN: There is one major benefit, I think, to the increase in carbon dioxide that everybody's concerned about, and that is plants grow much more effectively. They will grow . . . You can increase the carbon dioxide in greenhouses and you'll get plants to grow at a rate of two and three times what they normally do and they take much less water in order to be able to grow.

NARRATOR: In the documentary titled "The Great Global Warming Swindle," scientists question today's popular theory on global warming. Dr. Tim Ball, a prominent climatologist from Canada, has received several death threats for speaking out on his views regarding the causes of climate change.

DR. TIMOTHY BALL: All scientists should be skeptics. All scientists should question anything and challenge all the time. Where it became really personal and nasty was when we were called "deniers"—and of course, all of the holocaust connotations of that term, which is really an obscenity. What's amusing about it is we're called "climate change deniers" when in fact my whole career has been going around the country saying the climate changes all the time.

GEORGE H. TAYLOR: Just by saying that I don't think that humans control climate, I am painted into a corner and somehow cast as a demon by one side and as a hero by the other. And I think I'm not really a hero nor a demon, but I'm just a scientist who studies what he sees and tries to report on it.

DR. JAY WILE: The radical environmentalist movement, one of the key problems that they have is, in order to make some of the statements they're saying, they have to basically ignore science. And if you're trying to take care of the earth, if you're trying to make sure its ecosystems are working correctly and so forth, then in the end you have to look at science; it's our only tool for knowing what's wrong with the earth, how to fix it, and so forth. Time and time again though, these radical environmentalists have to actually ignore the science in order to say what they have to say.

DR. E. CALVIN BEISNER: If you can persuade people that this great catastrophe is on the horizon, you can promote that agenda. And the easiest way, it seems, to persuade people is not to argue the evidence.

A BIBLICAL PERSPECTIVE

DR. E. CALVIN BEISNER: From the typical environmentalist's perspective, the best environment is nature untouched by human hands. That's not a biblical understanding at all. The Bible says that when God created man, He told him, He gave him a commission, to multiply, to fill up the earth, to subdue it, and to rule over it. When He placed him in the Garden of Eden, which was not the entire planet, He told him to cultivate and guard the Garden.

NARRATOR: And in Romans 1:25, the apostle Paul warns us against those who have exchanged the truth of God for a lie and worshiped and served created things rather than the Creator.

GEORGE H. TAYLOR: One of the things that I see happening with a lot of groups and a lot of people is what we call pantheism, and that's worshiping the creation. You know, one of the terms we have in the northwest is "tree hugger," which is not necessarily a bad term but I think it represents the fact that often people tend to worship God's creation and not worship the Creator Himself.

ALTERNATIVE THEORIES

DR. ROY SPENCER: I think there's probably something going on with sunlight that we don't understand.

NARRATOR: Dr. Roy Spencer, former senior scientist of climate studies at NASA's Marshall Space Flight Center and principal research scientist at the University of Alabama, suggests solar variability drives climate change.

DR. ROY SPENCER: It only takes a small change in the radiation to do what we're seeing. I mean, we're only talking about two-tenths of a degree C warming every decade, and that's considered a lot of warming, and it turns out that the change in either sunlight or infrared radiation that you need to get that is really tiny.

MICHAEL J. OARD: We know that there are these temperature fluctuations and we know that these temperatures fluctuations, with the medieval warm period and the Little Ice Age, have nothing to do with the increase in carbon dioxide because carbon dioxide didn't start increasing til about 1850. We know that based on statistical correlations of the amount of solar radiation and the sunspot cycle correlated with the temperature cycle since about 1900. For instance, between 1880 and 1910, the temperature just oscillated; it didn't really change a lot. In 1910 to 1940, it went up a lot and then it peaked, and then it went down from 1940 to about 1975. It actually cooled and then it's been going up from since 1975 to the present day. So when you check the sunspot cycle, the sunspot cycle hit that right on where it got the warming going to 1910 to 1940 and it caught the cooling trend into the 1970s. And then it's been going up slightly ever since. So it's correlated with that. Well, the carbon dioxide trend was pretty flat, going up only slowly since the industrial revolution til after World War II.

DR. JASON LISLE: We know that sunspots, when there are more sunspots, the solar intensity is greater and so it's reasonable to conclude that the earth probably experiences larger temperatures during those time periods. Of course, it's not all that simple because the earth has its own system and it's a very complex climate as well. And so just because you turn up the sun's intensity doesn't necessarily mean the earth's overall temperature will increase as a result of it, but that would be the most natural conclusion.

DR. LARRY VARDIMAN: One of the explanations for global warming is that it's not a long term trend, but a fluctuation in short-term. And in fact we already know that there are such fluctuations, they're called the El Niño Southern Oscillation. This occurs in the South Pacific (or in the Pacific Ocean) about every seven to ten years. We have the La Niña— produces more precipitation and severe weather particularly along the west coast but it affects the whole globe. This short-term fluctuation of every seven to ten years is just an example of the periodicities that typically occur in climate. There are some that are on the order of twenty to fifty years. There are others on the order of a hundred years. There's even some on the order of a thousand years. We know, for example, if you go back a thousand years ago, we were in what was called the Climatic Optimum. That is, it was warm for about 400 years—from a thousand years ago to about 600 years ago. And then there was a period for about another 300 years in which it was cold, called the Maunder Minimum.

DR. JASON LISLE: Well, the Maunder Minimum is a period of several decades that was in the late 1600s and just into the very early 1700s, where there were very few spots on the sun. And in fact, there were about a thousand times fewer spots than there would be in a typical decade today, where we might have several thousand in a decade, there you might have five. So it's an enormous difference and it turns out that this corresponds with the peak of what we call the Little Ice Age, a period of decreased temperatures on the earth. It happened at around that time— actually it lasted a little bit longer than that but the peak of that was during the Maunder Minimum—and so it's been suggested, I think it's a reasonable inference, that perhaps the fewer sunspots, and therefore the sun having a lower intensity overall, has in fact caused the lower temperatures on the earth. And therefore, the fact that we have more sunspots today might be at least partly responsible for why we have increased temperatures today.

GEORGE H. TAYLOR: One of the really exciting new discoveries in my opinion is the effect of changes in sunlight on cosmic rays. It's something that's been studied for less than ten years. The leader in this is a scientist named Svensmark, who's Danish, and what he found is that when sunlight changes, it really affects the cosmic rays that hit the earth's atmosphere. When the sun is more intense, the solar wind generated by the sun tends to sweep away cosmic rays—make them less common. The main effect of cosmic rays in the earth's atmosphere is to create clouds, because cosmic rays actually cause condensation of water. So when there are more cosmic rays there tend to be more clouds; fewer cosmic rays, they're associated with fewer clouds. Now when the sun is brighter, sweeping away the cosmic rays, it really means less cloud cover and we can see the cloud cover really matching up nicely and very systematically with these changes in sunlight. So what you get when the sun is brighter is you get kind of the double effect—a little bit more radiation but probably, more significantly, less cloud cover. And we know that clouds have a huge effect on climate but it's one that has never really been systematically modeled or simulated in climate models.

WHAT ABOUT GREENHOUSE GASES?

NARRATOR: The majority of media attention has been focused on the need to reduce greenhouse gases in the atmosphere, such as carbon dioxide or CO_2, to stop global warming.

DR. ROY SPENCER: One of the big misconceptions about greenhouse gases is that carbon dioxide is the main one, and that's not true. The earth's natural greenhouse effect is mostly due to water vapor and clouds.

NARRATOR: In fact, 95% of greenhouse gases are actually water vapor, and the input of CO_2 by humans into the earth's atmosphere is miniscule.

GEORGE H. TAYLOR: What tends to happen with the climate models is they hold most things constant. We don't know how the El Niño and La Niña are going to change in the future so we'll just kind of leave them out. We don't know about sunspot cycles, long term and short term, so we leave that out. And we don't know how things like land use change are going to have an effect, so we leave those out. And what we're left with is really changes in greenhouse gases, especially carbon dioxide.

DR. TIMOTHY BALL: The focus is just on CO_2, which is a very small part of it. The sun explains virtually all of the temperature change that we're seeing.

NARRATOR: Notice the correlation between solar warming and the earth's temperature changes over the past century. In spite of these findings, Dr. Ball says that the funding that supports the theory of man-made global warming has created an industry that has generated a truth of its own.

DR. TIMOTHY BALL: In the US, it's a hundred billion at last count, federal money going to funding, trying to prove the theory. And of course, that's completely against the scientific method because the scientific method tries to disprove a theory not prove it. And so you're not only funding only one side of it, but you're also thwarting how science should properly work.

GEORGE H. TAYLOR: One of my favorite scientists was the late Richard Feynman, who was a premier physicist in the US. Feynman said, "The finest scientists are always trying to prove themselves wrong." What I really see in science is often the reverse of that. People are trying to prove themselves right and they seem to grasp at things that will prove their point.

DR. KEN CHILTON: The funding, for government funding, for grants, is skewed now towards those who believe that climate change is a problem. After all, why would you fund research for something that's not a problem? And so there has been a war chest built up for those who supposedly represent the consensus view.

NARRATOR: Dr. Ken Chilton is an associate professor of environmental economics at Lindenwood University in St. Charles, Missouri. He warns that if we implement a reduction in oil use it could cost us dearly in the long run.

DR. KEN CHILTON: What would the gas prices look like if we had to try to reduce oil use, coal use, and our energy use in our house? Coal is the primary source for producing electricity in this country. Well it would impoverish even a rich country like the United States. The rich countries of the world would not be able to help the developing countries because we would become like the developing countries.

DR. LARRY VARDIMAN: The suggestion has been made that we need to reduce carbon dioxide input to the atmosphere below what we had back in 1990, even cutting it maybe by 50% below that. To do that would take a major percentage of the economy out of our culture. We could spend 50% of our annual product, economic product, to be able to make that kind of an effect. That is a major commitment to do that. But probably more important is would it do any good? And I'm convinced that it wouldn't. For one thing, is I don't think the carbon dioxide increase that we have measured is producing that big of an effect. I think the primary increase is due to something different—the variation in the electromagnetic fields on the sun. And for us to spend a major percentage of our economy to try to reduce carbon dioxide, when it's probably not the main cause and probably wouldn't have a major effect, I think would be a major mistake.

DR. TIMOTHY BALL: People that have a political agenda see it as a very nice vehicle to push their own agenda. It's logical to want to be a good citizen of earth. We are citizens of earth but you don't do it when you are being pressured by fear and also when you're being exploited because of your lack of understanding.

DR. ROY SPENCER: One of the justifications for doing something about global warming is it will help the poor because the poor supposedly are at the greatest risk from global warming. The truth is, is what the poor are at risk of is dying from poverty and disease as a result of poverty. And so what we need . . . they need to use more energy and, of course, to have the freedom to have free markets and all that to get themselves out of poverty.

NARRATOR: According to poverty.org, hunger alone kills over nine million people each year.

DR. LARRY VARDIMAN: One of the unintended consequences of trying to do an all out war on global warming is that it is going to cause the developing countries not to be able to develop as they need. They are in poverty at this point and one of the best chances they have for being able to get out of poverty is to be able to have the technology applied to agriculture, and to be able to get power, to be able to put in technology into small villages, and so on. If in fact we enforce the same criteria that we're trying to enforce upon ourselves in developed countries, it's going to stop the developing countries from growing at all. And that is really a major catastrophe, I think, for these poor developing countries.

DR. E. CALVIN BEISNER: If then we're going to reduce CO_2 emissions significantly in an attempt to fight global warming, we're going to have to greatly increase the costs of fossil fuels, which in turn will diminish economic production and particularly diminish the rate of economic development, especially in poor countries. The result of that is going to be that we condemn people in poor countries—the roughly two billion of the people in this world who live right now without electricity to their homes, without pure drinking water, or sewage sanitation. We will condemn them to decades or generations more of the great poverty in which they live and the disease, the high death rates, that they suffer right now because of that.

DR. KEN CHILTON: Poor people actually do the most environmental harm. Why? Because it's about survival. If I have to go cut down a tree in order to have firewood and I have to have firewood to burn in my little house to make food, then I'm going to do that, if I'm poor. I have to; I have no choice. But if you're wealthy enough you've got more alternatives, more ways to address a problem. If you're poor, you're just going to wind up being victimized by things like hurricanes, by floods, by ice storms.

DR. JOHN CHRISTY: Believers should understand the great blessings that we have achieved through these past few thousand years and that gives us the ability to enhance human life, which I think is a command in Scripture.

POLITICS AND PEOPLE

NARRATOR: In Matthew 25:40 the Scripture says, "The king will reply, 'I tell you the truth. Whatever you did for one of the least of these brothers of mine, you did for me.'"

NARRATOR: Many evangelical Christians have recently become concerned with environmental issues because of a proper desire to be good stewards of God's creation. But does the modern environmental movement uphold the biblical view of the environment?

DR. RICHARD LAND: It's pretty clear in the Bible that the earth is the Lord's and that human beings are put in charge as God's vicars, as his vice regents. And we are to be there seeking to exercise stewardship responsibility. That means to use the earth and its resources in renewable ways that benefit human beings without desecrating.

NARRATOR: Dr. Richard Land is the president of the Ethics and Religious Liberty Commission of the Southern Baptist Convention.

DR. RICHARD LAND: In Genesis chapter 2, Adam was put into the Garden to keep it and to till it. To keep it means to guard it and to protect it. To till it means to cause it bring forth its fruit, to develop it. For what purpose? For human good. And in

Genesis chapter 1, the Bible tells us that we are given dominion, and the word dominion there is a strong word—dominion over the earth.

NARRATOR: Indeed, in Genesis 1:26 we read, "Then God said, 'Let us make man in our image according to our likeness. Let them have dominion over the fish of the sea, over the birds of the air, and over the cattle, over all the all earth and over every creeping thing that creeps on the earth.'" Yet the modern environmental movement often seems to be driven by a much different view.

DR. RICHARD LAND: They tend to look upon human beings as the enemy of nature. E.O. Wilson, the Harvard biologist, in his new book, talks about human beings as an alien species, and human beings as an alien species having a negative impact on nature. I'm sorry, human beings are not an alien species to nature as created by God.

DR. JAY WILE: If you truly believe that everything we see around us is the result of evolution, then you believe random chance is the main architect. It's been guided by natural selection but the architect itself is random chance. Well, random chance is a terrible designer of things, so you would expect anything that random chance is able to cobble together is going to be incredibly fragile and not work very well. So if you believe that, you will probably believe then that the earth's ecosystems are incredibly fragile and have to be worried over every second of every day. If you believe, instead, that this is all the result of very powerful, very intelligent designer, you figure the designer has put in feedback mechanisms and fail safes to keep the earth robust as it changes over the course of time. So, under that scenario, you wouldn't be so worried about the fragileness of earth. You'd want to protect earth and take care of earth the way you take care of any fine gift you're given. But in the end you wouldn't think of it as fragile, you'd think of it as something that's robust that I simply need to be a steward of.

DR. LARRY VADIMAN: God gave us this earth in which we live as a resource, which doesn't mean that we should abuse it; we need to be very careful how we use it, but we are to use it. There are some who would take an extreme position and say that we shouldn't use this world, this atmosphere, the climate, soils, forests, or anything—that it should be left pristine. That's not the case. But we need to be very careful as stewards, that we don't abuse it.

Dr. JOHN CHRISTY: I've often talked to environmentalists who truly have the view that humans are bad for the planet, the planet would be better off without humans, and so it fits their view of what can we do to cease development, to help human life expand? They see those as bad things. I think the number one thing evangelical Christians should remember is what is at the peak of the pyramid in terms of creation? And if you read Genesis especially, you'll see that human life is at the peak of the pyramid and it is human life that has the greatest value in terms of what you see in creation. And, therefore, what you do to preserve, protect, grant security, and health to, in terms of human life is the number one thing you can do.

DR. JAY WILE: People live longer and live healthier in developed countries. So if we delay Africa even by 10 years in their development, in the end that's going to be 10 years of bodies we leave behind and that has to be figured into any proposal. How many bodies is it going to pile up in order for this proposal to come to fruition?

NARRATOR: Experts point out that well-meaning Christians should be very careful when advocating environmental policies, even with the best of intentions.

GEORGE H. TAYLOR: Science lives with uncertainty. Policy and politics don't have that. Policy and politics are black and white. They're yes or no. Do we pass the bill or do we not? Do we vote "aye" or "nay?" And so that's what policy makers have to do based on the input from scientists. As I see it, some scientists have fallen into the trap of treating climate change as a black and white issue, and it isn't.

DR. KEN CHILTON: Unfortunately, what looks and appears good often times to policy makers has unintended consequences that are quite tragic. A good example: the whole environmental movement kicked off for us anyway, in the Western world, with Rachel Carson's book *Silent Spring*.

NARRATOR: Carson's 1962 book claimed that the pesticide DDT caused cancer and threatened certain bird species, but DDT had also been extraordinarily successful in combating malaria-carrying mosquitoes with the World Health Organization estimating it saved half a billion lives.

DR. KEN CHILTON: What happens with DDT sprayed in a home or hut in Africa is the mosquitoes typically don't even want to enter the house. If they land on the wall of the house, they're going to die, but generally it just wards them off. And it has protection for almost six months—very inexpensive.

NARRATOR: In the years following World War II, malaria was nearly eradicated in countries where DDT was used. But Carson's book ultimately spawned a worldwide moratorium on the pesticide. More than four decades later, most of her claims about DDT have been disproved, yet malaria, spread by mosquitoes, is again one of the leading causes of death in underdeveloped countries, killing more than a million people a year.

GEORGE H. TAYLOR: There does tend to be a habit for the media to use sensation, and I think a lot of scientists have gotten caught up in that. They will proclaim things that prove a point that tend to be spectacular, and often the doomsayers are the ones that get the most attention. So when doom-saying turns out not to be true, you seldom get the retractions; you don't get the people saying, "Sorry, we were wrong," they just kind of move on to a different topic.

DR. KEN CHILTON: The unintended consequence? A huge rise in malarial deaths and malarial cases again in the parts of the world that are the poorest—in sub-Saharan Africa and elsewhere, I think we can safely say they were in the tens of millions. That's a lot of humanity. Yes, Christians should care about the environment just because we care about the Creator, but we do have to be careful.

NARRATOR: Many experts say the best thing we can do for the environment, while also benefiting marginalized peoples, is encourage economic growth.

DR. E. CALVIN BEISNER: Environmental protection is better done in wealthier societies than it is in poorer societies, which is why the greatest environmental disasters are all occurring in the poorest places in the world, not in the wealthiest places. If we want to protect the environment, we really need to promote the economic development of the poor.

NARRATOR: But much of the modern environmental movement is opposed to the solution as seen in the global warming controversy.

DR. KEN CHILTON: I've studied the environment for probably twenty years. I've studied climate change for fifteen and they're not easy topics. They've always got a hidden, unintended consequence to them generally that people don't think about.

DR. E. CALVIN BEISNER: There are some environmentalists who are just basically anti-capitalism, anti-political freedom, anti-wealth, anti-industrialization, and they see the promotion of fears about global warming as a way to serve their own agenda because if we can convince people that we must make drastic cuts in CO_2 emissions, well the only way to do that is to greatly reduce our use of fossil fuels.

DR. JAY WILE: We often hear people saying, "Even if we don't know that carbon dioxide buildup is causing global warning, we need to do something to stop it, just in case that's what could be caused in fifty or a hundred years." The problem with that attitude is if I do something to try and reduce carbon dioxide levels now, people will die as a result. For example, if the United States signed the Kyoto Protocol, which is supposed to help us reduce greenhouse gas emissions, then in the end our cost of heating oil would go up. As heating oil costs go up, poor people tend to turn off the heat in the winter. And every year poor people, especially poor elderly people, die because they can't afford to heat their homes. Now is it really worth sacrificing these people for something we don't even know is real?

BIBLICAL ENVIRONMENTALISM

DR. RICHARD LAND: The question is whether or not evangelicals allow themselves to be manipulated, allow themselves to be duped, and what we are to do is to judge everything by the plumb line of the Word of God. And the Word of God in the first nine chapters of Genesis gives us the foundational planks of a biblical environmental ethic. And if you look at those you will find that they're considerably at odds with the modern radical environmentalist movement.

DR. JAY WILE: The Bible tells us that we have to reason. "Come let us reason together," says the Lord. So it's a Christian's responsibility to reason through these things. It's not enough simply to listen to the propaganda and believe it. We have to actually reason through it. I think that's actually a scriptural imperative for us to be "thoughtful" about these kinds of things. So, regardless of whether it's real or not, we have to at least first reason through it to decide, and I think if we reason through it, we will come up, we will see some of these unintended consequences, and we can come up with ways of fixing those.

WHAT TO DO

MICHAEL J. OARD: I think Christians should apply 1 Thessalonians 5:21, which says, "Examine everything carefully but hold fast to that which is good." And that's been my research principle for 40 years. I believe in holding fast to that which is good—to the Bible as God's word, to Jesus as my Lord and Savior. But then I examine everything carefully, I don't think Jesus meant us to just accept everything that the world has out there from the environmental movement to a lot of different controversial issues, but we're to examine everything carefully. So based on that, I believe Christians should look at the data and examine this issue at more than the superficial level.

DR. LARRY VARDIMAN: I think one of the main things as Christians, we need not buy into a view point just because of the intensity of the argument.

DR. JASON LISLE: I think that Christians need to have a balanced view of global warming. On the one hand, it's something that we should be interested in, something that we should be concerned about but not overly worried about, because God has given us dominion over this earth. We're to be good stewards of it, and therefore, to care for it and that involves researching things to make sure that they're not going to be a problem. But at the same time, we know that God takes care of the earth as well and it's something . . . that it's self-maintaining to some extent, and it's not something that we should sort of jump on the bandwagon of all the people that have a lot of hype about this issue. I think we need to have a balanced approach as Christians.

DVD Transcript Biographies

Timothy F. Ball, PhD
Chairman of the Natural Resources Stewardship Project
PhD, Geography, University of London, 1983
MA, Geography, University of Manitoba, 1970
BA, University of Winnipeg

Dr. Timothy Ball wrote his doctoral thesis at the University of London using the remarkable records of the Hudson's Bay Company to reconstruct climate change from 1714 to 1952. He was a Professor of Geography at the University of Winnipeg from 1988 until his retirement in 1996. Dr. Ball has published numerous articles on climate change and its impact on the human condition. He has served on numerous committees at the federal, provincial, and municipal levels on climate, water resources, and environmental issues. Dr. Ball is currently working as an environmental consultant and public speaker based in Victoria, BC.

E. Calvin Beisner, PhD
National Spokesman for the Cornwall Alliance
BA, Interdisciplinary Studies in Religion and Philosophy, University of Southern California, 1978
MA, Society, International College, 1983
PhD, Scottish History, University of St. Andrews, 2003

E. Calvin Beisner is a founder of and the national spokesman for the Cornwall Alliance for Environmental Stewardship (formerly called the Interfaith Stewardship Alliance) and among the founding leaders of Holy Trinity Presbyterian Church in Broward

County, Florida. He is a former associate professor (2000–2007) of historical theology and social ethics at Knox Theological Seminary, where he taught church history, ethics, apologetics, logic, systematic theology, and non-Christian religions. Before Knox he taught for eight years at Covenant College as associate professor of interdisciplinary studies. He is also an adjunct fellow of the Acton Institute for the Study of Religion and Liberty; an adjunct scholar of the Committee for a Constructive Tomorrow; and a member of the advisory board of the Templeton Freedom Awards program of the Atlas Economic Research Foundation.

Kenneth W. Chilton, PhD
Director of the Institute for Study of Economics and the Environment
Associate Professor of Management at Lindenwood University
PhD, Business Administration, Washington University
MS, Management Science, Northwestern University
BS, Management Science, Northwestern University

Dr. Kenneth Chilton was a research faculty person and administrator at Washington University's Center for the Study of American Business for 23 years. He worked in private industry for nine years as an engineer, management science consultant, treasurer, and entrepreneur.

John R. Christy, PhD
Professor or Atmospheric Science
Director of the Earth System Science Center
University of Alabama in Huntsville
PhD, Atmospheric Sciences, University of Illinois, Champaign-Urbana, 1987
MS, Atmospheric Sciences, , University of Illinois, Champaign-Urbana, 1984
BA, Mathematics, California State University, Fresno, 1969

Dr. John R. Christy began studying global climate issues in 1987. In November 2000 Governor Don Siegelman appointed him to be Alabama's State Climatologist. In 1989 Dr. Roy W. Spencer, a NASA/Marshall scientist, and Christy developed a global temperature data set from microwave data observed from satellites beginning in 1979. For this achievement, the Spencer-Christy team was awarded NASA's Medal for Exceptional Scientific Achievement in 1991. In 1996, they were selected to receive a Special Award by the American Meteorological Society "for developing a global, precise record of earth's temperature from operational polar-orbiting satellites, fundamentally advancing our ability to monitor climate."

Dr. Christy has served as a Contributor (1992, 1994, and 1996) and Lead Author (2001) for the U.N. reports by the Intergovernmental Panel on Climate Change in which the satellite temperatures were included as a high-quality data set for studying global climate change. He has or is serving on five National Research Council panels or committees and has performed research funded by NASA, NOAA, DOE, DOT, and the State of Alabama and has published many articles including studies appearing in Science, Nature, Journal of Climate, and The Journal of Geophysical Research.

Richard D. Land, PhD
President of The Ethics & Religious Liberty
Commission
Southern Baptist Convention
PhD, Oxford University
ThM, New Orleans Baptist Theological
Seminary
BA, Princeton University

As host of *For Faith & Family, For Faith & Family's Insight,* and *Richard Land LIVE!* three nationally syndicated radio programs, Dr. Richard Land speaks passionately and authoritatively on the social, ethical, and public policy issues facing our country.

Dr. Land has contributed articles to both learned journals and popular periodicals and has served as contributing editor for the *Criswell Study Bible* and the *Believer's Study Bible.* He is a Southern Baptist minister, having been ordained since 1969. He has pastored Baptist churches in Texas, Louisiana and England. Dr. Land has also authored more than seven books on social, moral, and ethical concerns from a biblical perspective.

Jason Lisle, PhD
Speaker, Researcher, Writer
Answers in Genesis
BS, Physics & Astronomy, Ohio Wesleyan University, 1997
MS, Astrophysics, University of Colorado at Boulder, 1999
PhD, Astrophysics, University of Colorado at Boulder, 2004

Dr. Jason Lisle graduated *summa cum laude* from Ohio Wesleyan University where he double-majored in physics and astronomy, and minored in mathematics. He did graduate work at the University of Colorado where he earned a Master's degree and a PhD in Astrophysics. While there, Dr Lisle used the SOHO spacecraft to investigate motions on the surface of the sun as well as solar magnetism and subsurface weather. His thesis was entitled "Probing the Dynamics of Solar Supergranulation and its Interaction with Magnetism." He has also authored a number of papers in both secular and creation literature. Dr. Lisle is the author and programmer of several shows at the Stargazer's Planetarium at the Creation Museum near Cincinnati, Ohio.

Michael J. Oard
National Weather Service (Ret.)
BS, Atmospheric Science, University of Washington, 1969
MS, Atmospheric Science, University of Washington, 1973

Michael Oard has an MS in atmospheric science from the University of Washington and is now retired after working as a meteorologist with the US National Weather Service in Montana for 30 years. He is a prolific author, having written more than 40 technical papers and five books.

Roy W. Spencer, PhD
Principal Research Scientist
University of Alabama in Huntsville
BS, Atmospheric Sciences, University of Michigan, 1978
MS, Meteorology, University of Wisconsin in 1980
PhD, Meteorology, University of Wisconsin-Madison, 1982

Before becoming a Principal Research Scientist at the University of Alabama in Huntsville in 2001, Dr. Roy Spencer was a Senior Scientist for Climate Studies at NASA's Marshall Space Flight Center, where he and Dr. John Christy received NASA's Exceptional Scientific Achievement Medal for their global temperature monitoring work with satellites. Dr. Spencer is the U.S. Science Team leader for the Advanced Microwave Scanning Radiometer flying on NASA's Aqua satellite. His research has been entirely supported by U.S. government agencies: NASA, NOAA, and DOE.

George H. Taylor
President, Applied Climate Services
BA, Mathematics, U.C. Santa Barbara, 1969
MS, Meteorology, University of Utah, 1975

George Taylor, former Oregon State climatologist, retired as head of the Oregon Climate Service at Oregon State University in 2008. Prior to joining Oregon State University in 1989, Mr. Taylor operated his own consulting business in Santa Barbara,

California. Previously he was employed as a meteorologist by North American Weather Consultants and Environmental Research and Technology.

Mr. Taylor is past president of the American Association of State Climatologists. He is a member of the American Meteorological Society and has received certification as a Certified Consulting Meteorologist by the Society. Mr. Taylor has published over 200 reports, symposium articles, and journal articles.

Larry Vardiman, PhD
Professor of Atmospheric Science and Chair of the Department of Astro-geophysics
Institute for Creation Research
PhD, Atmospheric Science, Colorado State University, 1974
MS, Atmospheric Science, Colorado State University, 1972
BS, Meteorology, St. Louis University, 1967
BS, Physics, University of Missouri, 1965

Dr. Larry Vardiman is a member of the American Meteorological Society and has authored numerous technical papers and books including overseeing the editing of the book, *Radioisotopes and the Age of the Earth*. Much of Dr. Vardiman's scientific contributions have been in the areas of cloud seeding, ice crystal growth and evolution, the age of the earth's atmosphere, ice sheet formation during the Ice Age, and catastrophic hurricane formation. Dr. Vardiman also worked for the United States Air Force as an Officer with the Air Weather Service in the Aerospace Modification Division at Scott Air Force Base. He was part of the Summer Research Program with the Air Force and was appointed to the Air Force Geophysics Lab in Boston, Massachusetts, during the summer of 1985.

While obtaining his PhD, Dr. Vardiman served as a research assistant at Colorado State University's Department of Atmospheric

Science (1970–74) and served as a consulting Meteorologist at Western Scientific Services (1973–74). After obtaining his degree, he stayed in Colorado and served as a Consultant to the Colorado Governor's Advisory Panel on Weather Modification and as Meteorologist for the Bureau of Reclamation, Division of Atmospheric Resources Research in Denver, CO (1974–82).

Dr. Jay Wile
President, Apologia Educational Ministries
PhD, Nuclear Chemistry, University of Rochester,
1989
BS Chemistry, University of Rochester, 1985

Dr. Jay Wile is a member of the American Chemical Society and the American Association for the Advancement of Science. Dr. Wile's teaching experience includes the University of Rochester, Indiana University, Ball State University, and The Indiana Academy for Science (a high school for gifted and talented students). Dr. Wile has published more than 25 technical papers in scientific journals.

Providing answers to your entire family all year long!

Join the thousands of subscribers who enjoy quarterly issues of this fast-growing, creation-based worldview magazine from Answers in Genesis. Each issue is packed with relevant articles, stunning photos, and graphics that reveal the latest creation science news while equipping you and your family for the culture war in today's society.